Effective Leadership Strategies for Women

A Practical Guide for Women to Successfully Influence, Motivate and Inspire

Sabina Mitchell

Table of Contents

the use of the information contained within this document, including, but not limited to, errors, omissions, or inaccuracies.

To P.E. Bennett,

For being the woman who has consistently influenced, motivated and inspired me so much throughout my life.

Preface

Since 1972, women have gone from making up 18% of the managerial workforce to more than half.[1] With this rise in women leaders, challenges have risen as well. Whether dealing with cultural norms stemming from eras from the past or modern-day, tests of leadership - women face a work world that requires a constant development of skills and strategies to prove themselves as competent leaders and educated managers. They must face all this while at the same time mitigate the recurrent battles of womanhood. Throughout this book, you will be introduced to the unique barriers women in leadership often endure and the causes of these challenges. You will also attain actionable strategies in order to counter these challenges.

This book will also reveal approaches to improve the support of women who are a part of marginalized groups and explores inclusive policy change affecting women.

Some specific dilemmas that women in leadership face such as the "double-bind dilemma" and the "confidence gap" will also be explored in-depth as well as emotional intelligence and resilience.

The "How-Tos": Practical Strategies

---

[1] U.S. Women in Business. (2008). Catalyst. Retrieved May 11, 2008, from http://www.catalyst.org/ publication/132/us-women-in-business

9

You will discover strategies to overcome feelings of "only-ness," when you are the only one of your gender in the room. There will be hopeful and constant advocacy for partnerships, mentorships, and allies when facing the ceaseless struggles that women in the workplace face. Finally, the examination of networking and negotiation strategies will embolden women leaders to look to their resources, to self-advocate, and to inspire other women when looking for advancement in their careers.

The Gender Spectrum

To Make Things Clear...

Though sex is a biological label that drives much of people's daily lives, it is gender that actually plays a much more critical factor in the way women are recognized in leadership. Sex and gender are not equivalent. A person's gender is an intricate and intimate interconnected relationship between social gender, body and identity. [2] And the identity of any individual on this gender spectrum will experience some barriers when entering a leadership position regardless of where on that spectrum they lie. The strategies discussed within the following chapters will

---

[2]"Understanding Gender," Gender Spectrum, accessed October 21, 2020. https://genderspectrum.org/articles/understanding-gender

be tailored towards women and those who identify as such; however, these strategies will also benefit the agendered, non-binary, genderfluid, and/or genderqueer.

This book will build the case for an approach that is specific and geared towards the experience of identifying women in positions of leadership in the modern workplace. These strategies must be specific to women because the context in which women navigate their daily lives, deal with coworkers and subordinates, provide feedback and build resilience is distinct and needs to be unique to their developmental needs.

Chapter 1: INFLUENCE: How to Strengthen Your Impact

Overview

Though significant strides have been made towards gender equality and creating a safer space for women everywhere, there is still a disparity between men and women, especially for those in leadership positions. Women should learn the skills to lead themselves and other women towards a modern workplace that focuses on equality, safety, and ongoing development. But prior to garnering these skills, we must first consider what drives women to leadership and what leadership traits you can use to your own advantage. Following this, we can then discuss the importance of mental toughness, resilience and emotional intelligence in the development of strong leadership.

Leadership Traits

Emotional Intelligence – a secret weapon that every effective leader uses

Commitment, inspiration, communication - these may be some traits that people first think of when they consider what effective leadership truly is. Yet, there are also certain "must-have" qualities - characteristics that individuals look for in their own managers and bosses that motivate them to work diligently and effectively. Perhaps one of the most important qualities that is often not discussed is the range of a leader's emotional intelligence. But how is the regulation of emotions measured?

The Trait Meta Mood Scale (TMMS) was designed for exactly this purpose - to determine a person's tendency to regulate their moods and emotions and to discriminate between them, indicating how people's different reactions to mood and emotional changes can affect their lives. [3] The TMMS consists of 48 different items on a 5-point likert-like scale it includes traits like attention, empathy, and self-control. More specifically, it measures a person's capacity to pay *attention* and recognize their emotional states, the ability to *clarify* the differences between feelings and understand them, and a person's ability to *repair* and regulate their moods. [4]

Attention. Clarity. Repair.

Recently, this ability to pay attention, to clarify and to repair emotions has become increasingly popular as a way to measure effective leadership and interpersonal skills. If a leader is unable to improve their emotional intelligence, they will have difficulty not only

---

[3] Peter Salovey et al., "Emotional attention, clarity and repair: Exploring emotional intelligence using the trait meta-mood scale." *J.W. Pennebaker (Ed.), Emotion, Disclosure and Health,* (1995): 125-154. American Psychological Association. https://doi.org/10.1037/10182-006

[4] Julie Fitness and Marie Curtis. "Emotional Intelligence and the Trait Meta-Mood Scale: Relationships with Empathy, Attributional Complexity, Self-control, and Responses to Interpersonal Conflict." *E-Journal of Applied Psychology 1* (2005): 5. 10.7790/ejap.v1i1.9

recognizing their own needs but also the needs and expectations of those they lead. If a leader cannot regulate by reacting emotionally to mistakes or sudden profit loss - they may present unfiltered emotions to their employees that inevitably cause distrust and concern in their workspace. Not to mention seriously jeopardizing work relationships.

Women have been proved to score higher on emotional intelligence and empathy tests. [5] So, does this automatically make women better leaders? Not necessarily. However, there was a study done in 2005 by Julie Fitness and Marie Curtis observing the TMMS and gender and how it affects the way people deal with interpersonal conflict and relationships. Fitness and Curtis found that, even though the study was not specifically addressing differences in gender, women scored significantly higher scores in empathy, constructive responses, task-oriented coping, and emotion-oriented coping. And that gender explained over a 10% variance in functional responses to interpersonal conflict. In addition, "the tendency to use complex reasoning when thinking about the causes of people's behaviour" (Fitness & Curtis, 2005) was also more strongly associated with being female.

This topic will be discussed more in the upcoming section as emotional intelligence. This is a widely overlooked trait of what makes effective leaders with

---

[5] Nicola S. Schutte et al., "Development and Validation of a Measure of Emotional Intelligence." *Personality and individual differences 25,* no. 2 (1998): 167–177. https://doi.org/10.1016/S0191-8869(98)00001-4

women having a clear advantage in this category.

Wait, We Can't Forget "The Big C"

Inspirational author Catherine Pulsifer said, "Communication is one of the most important skills you require for a successful life." Even if women have high emotional intelligence or an endless amount of empathy, if you are not able to communicate with your colleagues, clients and friends and family, you may be doing yourself a disservice. Communication is often viewed as the most important skill in becoming a successful leader. As a leader, you must be able to provide clear expectations, and feedback. You must be able to coach and delegate. Leaders will likely have to speak publicly and hold meetings - all these skills stem from the big C: Communication.

Integrity is Integral

In addition to communication and emotional intelligence, another trait that may be a blind spot for large corporations is integrity. Though the importance of it may be obvious this is especially important for top-level executives and board members. In fact, the Center for Creative Leadership determined that "integrity was the most important trait for a top-level executive's performance." [6]

---

[6] "The Irony of Integrity: Character Traits Leaders Need," *Center for Creative Leadership*, accessed October 23, 2020, https://www.ccl.org/articles/white-papers/the-irony-of-integrity-a-study-of-the-character-strengths-of-leaders/

Integrity is an essential trait to have when deciding what actions need to be taken. But the Center for Creative Leadership also determined that there is somewhat of an issue with the integrity development in top-level executives because of the nature of the traits in middle-management. While integrity is the most important for the higher-ups, they determined that social intelligence was the essential skill for middle-managers. Women should have an advantage with this since they are able to handle interpersonal relationships better due to their empathy and constructive responses. Could this have to do with why nowadays society is beginning to see more women in middle-management, yet CEOs and top-level executives are still widely men? This is not to say, in any capacity, that women are lacking in integrity but rather they may lack the opportunity to demonstrate the perceived integrity that is required for high-level management. So, as the Center for Creative Leadership determined, there should be a focus on the development of social intelligence and integrity when individuals are in positions of middle-management to prevent a lack of this crucial leadership skill.

Emotional intelligence, communication and integrity - these are the three traits that should be viewed as the most important for women in leadership. These are the characteristics that have been proven to be most successful for leaders.

The Psychology of Women as Leaders

Women in leadership will face many personal and professional challenges throughout the lifespan of any given career. Some of these could set you back or cause doubt in your own skills and aptitude. That's why it is of the utmost importance that women develop three things: mental toughness, resilience and emotional intelligence. The last of which was already touched upon, but will be further explored in detail as it relates to how emotional intelligence leads to a higher-level of self-assurance and self-control.

Mental Toughness

Firstly, mental toughness: grit, determination, perseverance, and endurance are all essential to women, in the face of a patriarchal society. Quite often, this concept is used when talking about athletes. Mental toughness is the capacity to deliver work to a high standard on a regular basis even though you are experiencing a variety of situational demands. However, this is not just for athletes. Let's take the Relentless Athletics Model and apply this to women in leadership: According to Kirkpatrick, mental toughness development is the combination of three major factors, the athlete, their relationships and their experiences spanning over the period of their career.

Positioning Yourself for Higher Standards

Now, position yourself within this same model, taking the place of the athlete, as a woman in leadership. In order to build mental toughness, you must first have an internal motive for success whether that is to improve your communication skills, your relationships with your employees and/or clients or perhaps just to be a better leader. There must be some type of *desire* to improve in order to develop mental toughness.

In this same vein, as "the athlete," you must also be coachable. You must be willing to learn and reframe experiences as learning experiences.

The next factor that Kirkpatrick touches on is an athlete's relationships, typically athlete-coach. For women in leadership these relationships may be manager-to-employee or colleague-to-colleague, it may also include company and workplace culture and relationships at home. Kirkpatrick continues to break the types of support you, as the 'athlete' can receive into four categories: emotional, esteem, informational and tangible.

- **Emotional Support** - Ensuring that your needs are met and that you feel cared for and are valued in your workplace. This may also mean providing this same support to your employees and receiving this support from your own leaders.

- **Esteem Support** - Knowing your worth, your skills and what makes you a good and effective leader.

- **Informational Support** - Discovering new strategies and information on how to be the best leader you can be. You have already pursued this type of support by picking up this book.

- **Tangible Support** - Improving your performance as a leader through physical things like planners and organizers, updated technology and coffee. Yes, coffee!

The final factor that Kirkpatrick presents is experiences which will take up the majority of your careers as women in leadership. This may include several things such as opportunities to overcome failure when a pitch does not land or when sales suddenly drop, challenging environments and employees, and exposure to critical events such as an employment review that will foster the ability to adapt, to change, and to improve as a leader. [7] The ability to adapt is at the heart of the next necessary psychological development for women leaders: resilience.

Resilience

Perhaps you've heard of the concept of resilience - the ability to remain strong in the face of ever-changing circumstances and high demands. It ties in with mental toughness and emotional intelligence, placing itself as the core mental skill to be developed as a woman in leadership. Because it is not only the ability to remain strong and steadfast when under pressure, but it is also the ability to remain flexible and use that adversity to your advantage.

---

[7] Julia J. Kirkpatrick, "Mental Toughness and Female Athletes," last modified May 13, 2019, https://www.relentlessathleticsllc.com/education/2019/05/mental-toughness-and-female-athletes

If you already feel that you are running on empty, it may be difficult to even imagine sustaining energy through adversity and even more difficult to imagine challenging that adversity, rebounding and then finding success. It's not uncommon for women to get burnt-out. It's downright normal. And this is why the development of resilience is absolutely essential for women leaders because of the rebound factor: getting back to operating at your best.

There are four strategies you can try to assist with building resilience. The first is knowing who you are. In order to begin building the skill to be strong in the face of dispiriting challenges, you must know what aspects may lead to those challenges in the first place. What sets you off? Is it disorganization? Poor time-management? What do you truly value in yourself and also in your employees? At your core, you must begin to prioritize your values.

Also, when getting to know yourselves as leaders, as women you should begin addressing your responses to past challenges and situations. Do you recognize what drives your thoughts and emotions? It should be considered that building up self-control and resilience does not mean that you should not be emotional and express yourself. Women leaders are often viewed as "overemotional" due to gender biases and stereotypes. These reflections may help you know and recognize reactions and experiences that may be limiting the growth of personal resilience.

Based on the Ladder of Inference by Jonathan Levene, women may want to consider a few things to answer the question above. The data you observed, the selected data from that observation, personal and cultural meanings, making assumptions based on the meanings, drawing conclusions, adopting beliefs about the world and taking action based on those beliefs. For example, if you have had negative experiences with a client from a specific company on more than one occasion you may begin to generalize from those experiences and have them affect your beliefs about that company and in turn, your actions. [8]You must be able to step out of these generalizations and out of this ladder of inference in order to consider other possibilities and understand what is driving your thoughts, emotions and actions and finally, knowing and understanding yourself as a leader and as a woman.

The second strategy that will help build resilience is having a strong purpose. This purpose is what drives your motivation and pushes you to keep going when challenges seem overwhelming and hopeless. Two questions to consider are:

- What in your work do you care deeply about?
- Even in the face of resistance, what maintains your hold on your values and principles?

Finding a purpose that truly motivates you is not an easy task. Helping others is one of the most common strategies that resilient people use. Not only is it helpful but volunteering or supporting a friend can

---

[8] Jonathan Leven, "Solving the Problems with Problem-Solving Meetings," *Professional Development* (blog), September 15, 2016, https://blog.dce.harvard.edu/professional-development/solving-problem-problem-solving-meetings

garner your sense of purpose, improve your self-worth and build connections. All of which build into the development of resilience.

In addition, the American Psychological Association details several helpful tips on the sense of purpose when building resilience such as moving towards your goals:

> Develop some realistic goals and do something regularly—even if it seems like a small accomplishment—that enables you to move toward the things you want to accomplish. Instead of focusing on tasks that seem unachievable, ask yourself, "What's one thing I know I can accomplish today that helps me move in the direction I want to go? [9]

Finally, in order to find your sense of purpose, look for opportunities of self-discovery that you may have experienced in current or past hardships. Resilience and purpose sprout from adversity and oppression. They lead to a development of self-worth and can increase your appreciation for your current position, workplace and future as a woman in leadership.

The next strategy that can build resilience is the fostering of compassion and generosity. In order to be compassionate towards those you lead, you must first be compassionate towards yourself. Think of the last time you experienced failure or perceived yourself as

---

[9] "Building your Resilience," *American Psychological Association,* 2012, https://www.apa.org/topics/resilience

weak - how compassionate were you towards yourself? Did you blame yourself or did you look to external factors? Women are notoriously harder on themselves when it comes to failure; this is even noted by professionals as "the confidence gap." Katty Kay and Claire Shipman discovered that women, no matter if they were incredibly successful or not, were in crisis - "a vast confidence gap that separates the sexes." (2014, Kay & Shipman)[10] With confidence comes the ability to be patient and compassionate with yourself and with others, it leads to the development of faith in your resilience and in your development as a leader. If your employees feel that they are supported through compassion it can lead to more honesty, patience and productivity in the workplace. In addition, being outwardly compassionate and generous has been linked to a personal payoff as it leads to better health and happiness in the long run. [11]

In 2004, a study was completed to gauge and understand resiliency in women leaders. As you work towards developing these skills in resiliency, you should look to your colleagues in leadership for examples and inspiration. When surveyed these women leaders shared a variety of challenges that they experienced that caused them to become more

---

[10] Katty Kay and Claire Shipman, "The Confidence Gap," The Atlantic (Atlantic Media Company, August 26, 2015), https://www.theatlantic.com/magazine/archive/2014/05/the-confidence-gap/359815/

[11]Mary Helen Immordino-Yang et al., "Neural correlates of admiration and compassion," *PNAS* 106, no. 19 (2009): 8021-8026. https://doi.org/10.1073/pnas.0810363106

resilient such as sickness and death in the family, discrimination issues and professional development issues related to schooling. After discussing these difficulties, these women shared how they viewed resilience and how they defined it. Janet Reno, Rose Tydus, Connie Mark, and Diane Wasserman Rubin all viewed it as the ability to bounce or snap back. One of the participants defined it as refusing to be a victim while another participant, Anna Escobedo Cabral, explained that it was about looking towards tomorrow, she said:

> I would say it is the ability to keep ever present the knowledge that the sun will rise tomorrow. I honestly believe...that unless you learn and can live by that philosophy, I think that the world will pull you down and suck you in. There are very, very difficult times, and I have recalled when I've gotten up and could not, as bright as the sun was shining, could not see it. You know, it was staring me in the face, and I was so sad and so beat, but in my mind, I told myself that it was still out there, and that if I could just get through the day, tomorrow would be better, and eventually there was a tomorrow that was better. [12]

The last step in building resilience is one that was previously mentioned: Emotional Intelligence. It

---

[12] Julia Baldwin et al., 2004 "Resilient Women Leaders: A Qualitative Investigation," Paper presented at *American Educational Research Association (AERA) Annual Meeting, San Diego, April 12- 16, 2004.* ERIC, https://files.eric.ed.gov/fulltext/ED500841.pdf

makes for great leaders and it is one of the most important factors in the development of the psychology of women in leadership.

Emotional Intelligence

As discussed earlier, in this aspect of psychology, women have a clear advantage. In 2016 in a study by Korn Ferry, women scored higher than men in all emotional intelligence categories except for one. High emotional intelligence has time and time again been shown to be a key predictor of the effectiveness in leaders. High emotional intelligence can lead to superior conflict management skills, inspirational leadership and unobjectionable empathy. In the Korn Ferry study, data was collected from 55,000 professionals across 90 countries between 2011 - 2015 from varied levels of management. Comparatively to men, women scored highest in empathy and self-awareness. The scores were closest on positive outlook. However, coaching & mentoring, teamwork, influence and adaptability were all categories in which women received higher scores. Self-control was the only score in which men rated equally with women. [13]

Women must begin to foster these inherent skills and further develop their emotional intelligence to become better leaders. Focusing on these developments and enhancing tools for self-control may assist with

[13] Monica Thakrar, "Why Women's Stronger Emotional Intelligence is a Big Leadership Advantage," *Développement Personnel* (blog), June 22, 2018, https://www.eveprogramme.com/36302/emotional-intelligence-monica-thakrar/

climbing the corporate ladder to top-level management or, at the very least, increase your management skills at your current level. The ability to control ourselves and our emotions is absolutely paramount to building resilience as a woman in leadership. After discovering where your challenges stem from, your sense of purpose and developing mental toughness, the next step is to build up a resilience toolbox. This is to ensure your emotions are in check to help you reach your goals, to strengthen your work relationships and ultimately, to better your resilience. Here are three techniques to add to your resilience toolbox and increase your self-control and emotional intelligence:

1. **Implementation Intention**

   Plan ahead and decide on an intention prior to a scenario that you know may test your self-control. If you already have your intention in mind, this can help you maintain willpower and self-control not unlike studying for a test or preparing a speech. For example, if you are heading into an employee review meeting, you may need to plan ahead and focus on your intention by either saying it to yourself or writing it down:

   "if they provide me with constructive feedback, I will not immediately react negatively. I will ask them for an explanation and write down their suggestions."

2. Meditation

Meditation seems to have almost become a buzzword in this day and age. But there is a reason it has garnered so much popularity and attention in recent years - because it works and because it is the ultimate test of self-control. It is the process of allowing thoughts to come and go without becoming fixated on ideas or reacting emotionally; it is an act of willpower. Make the time to meditate. Even if it is only 5 minutes a day, it can help build the muscles required for self-control so that next time a problem or stressor crops up in your workplace, you will be able to regulate your emotions spinning out of control and react to the situation by first *acknowledging* your emotions, and not necessarily acting on them.

3. Sleep

Sleep loss affects women more than men. [14] In fact, two-thirds of women reported that they had sleep problems at least a couple nights of the week in a 2007 survey by the National Sleep Foundation. [15] The side-effects of lack of sleep

---

[14] Edward C. Suarez, "Self-reported Symptoms of Sleep Disturbance and Inflammation, Coagulation, Insulin Resistance and Psychosocial Distress: Evidence for Gender Disparity," *Brain, Behavior, and Immunity 22,* no. 6 (2008): 960-8. doi:10.1016/j.bbi.2008.01.011

[15]"Summary of Findings," *National Sleep Foundation,* accessed October 27, 2020, https://www.sleepfoundation.org/wp-content/uploads/2018/10/Summary_Of_Findings-FINAL.pdf?x46574

are a loss in self-control, leading to less regulated emotions and our capacity to exert willpower is severely depleted. [16] So, it is essential for your own health and for the tone that you set in your workplace that you begin to develop habits of regular sleep. Set a consistent bedtime and an alarm set for the same time each morning to begin building these habits and setting yourself up for a successful day of self-control and achievements in emotional regulation.

Using the mentioned tools will lead to a development in self-control and ultimately resilience. There is power in resilience. You have the freedom to choose how you develop as a woman and as a leader. Resilience provides the choice of how you respond to your life. Frustrations and dissatisfaction will still occur, they will likely still be a daily occurrence for women in leadership, but it is your response to those frustrations that define you and set you apart as a highly effective leader.

---

[16] June J Pilcher et al., "Interactions Between Sleep Habits and Self-Control," *Frontiers in Human Neuroscience 9*, no. 284. (2015). doi:10.3389/fnhum.2015.00284

Chapter 2: NAVIGATE: How to Make Your Mark as a Trailblazer

It's a Man's World - or is it?

In building mental toughness and resilience, women in leadership will learn to better respond to challenges that they may experience in their careers. However, it is important that when dealing with these possible challenges that may arise both their root causes and the actionable strategies to manage them must be addressed. These challenges will be looked at through the lens of women in leadership and cover the following topics: traditional corporate settings and the "old boys' network," male-dominated industries, entrepreneurs, creative industries and speaking out against bias and harassment as a woman in leadership.

Corporate Setting

Historically, women in leadership have encountered gender-based barriers and challenges in a multitude of corporate settings and organizational structures. Many women have worked outside of what is commonly known as the "old boys' network". These informal networks were based on familiar social bonds between men that have been beneficial to their career advancement. These informal networks have not traditionally included women and consequently have inhibited and interfered with the advancement for women. These networks that exist in organizations are often long-standing and homogeneous in nature. This may present an inherent issue specifically for women as they may be required to navigate in an uncomfortable and unfamiliar social context established to benefit their male counterparts.

Promotions

Informal networking isn't the only factor that has historically excluded women from leadership, creating a challenge for women leaders. There are the promotions made within these corporate structures. Promotions require skills and experience; however, there may also be unclear parameters already set in place along with other unstated expectations which can make it yet more difficult for women to garner top-level executive positions. Furthermore, the ways to participate in professional development that may lead to promotions are at times under wraps or secretive in a typical corporate structure. This becomes a sort-of unspoken opportunity that causes even more ambiguity, leaving qualified women on the outside. Because of the limitations of women's support and potential essential relationships in the "old boys' network," they may experience a metaphorical wall between middle-management and upper-management often referred to as the "glass ceiling."

The "Glass-Cliff"

More recently and directly affecting women entering positions of leadership is the phenomenon known as the "glass cliffs." Many women who are able to push through the glass ceiling have been met with another barrier. Some women who are able to break through the challenges of male-dominated positions have experienced being promoted to high-risk positions that are leading workplaces that are already in crisis. [17] Women who are able to overcome all of these earlier barriers are seen as candidates that will be able to handle crisis and high-stress positions. Women become more likely to leave these positions that they have worked hard to obtain due to limited support networks and taxing roles.

Though argued that women in leadership were "wreaking havoc"[18] in the top 100 companies in Britain, it was later proven that women were more likely to be put into positions that were already associated with poor company performance. And when this newly-entered drawback for women was researched further by Ryan and Haslam in 2007, it was determined that over 50% of men went so far as to deny the existence of the glass cliff while less than 5% of women did so. Men were also more likely to question the validity of research on the glass cliff phenomenon and argue that men were the ones who were more likely to enter these types of precarious positions. Women explained this difference between the sexes by proposing factors such as sexism, lack of alternative opportunities and "the old boys' network"

[17]Michelle K. Ryan, S. Alexander Haslam and Tom Postmes, "Reactions to the Glass Cliff: Gender Differences in the Explanations for the Precariousness of Women's Leadership Positions," *Journal of Organizational Change Management 20*, no. 2 (2007): 182-197, 10.1108/09534810710724748

[18] Elizabeth Judge, "Women on Board: Help or Hindrance?" The Times, November 11, 2003, https://www.thetimes.co.uk/article/women-on-board-help-or-hindrance-2c6fnqf6fng

partisanship. Men explained these differences by questioning women's suitability for these strenuous leadership tasks, women's decision-making skills and factors that related to the company itself instead of gender. [19]

Conquering Corporate Culture Barriers

The situation may not be as dire as it seems. Now that you are aware of these challenges many women have encountered Here are some actionable strategies to overcome company culture barriers:

1. Make yourself aware and knowledgeable about the challenges that women experience in a traditional company culture. Being aware will help you navigate in ways that will make you more effective.

2. Identify your "water cooler" - Where are relationships and networking built in your workplace? Is it the actual water cooler or a place like the golf course or the restaurant across the street? Make yourself present in these areas to begin breaking through the old boys' club and building connections with colleagues.

3. Build your own girls' "club". Look for other women in leadership and female colleagues with potential. The old boys' club was not developed overnight; it is a structure of power

---

[19] Ryan, Haslam and Postmes, 187

that was built up over years of patriarchal hierarchy and resistance to change. Support from other women especially those in leadership is important but not essential. Women must build some type of alternative system to break through the conventions of company culture with or without the support from leadership and management. [20]

Therefore, even if you are to overcome the challenges of traditional company culture, earn a promotion, and break through the glass ceiling, you may encounter the dreaded glass cliff. In combination with social policy restrictions, this has led to some serious gender equality issues especially in fields like the police force, military, and other male-dominated industries.

Male-Dominated Industries

Though women have slowly begun to make themselves present in industries that are composed of more than 75% men, these occupations are particularly vulnerable to reinforcing gender stereotypes and present even further challenges to women in leadership. In 2018, it was determined that only 7.2% of women in the United States worked full-time in male-dominated industries.[21] Because there are fewer

[20] Liz Elting, "How to Navigate a Boys' Club Culture," Forbes, July 27, 2018, https://www.forbes.com/sites/lizelting/2018/07/27/how-to-navigate-a-boys-club-culture/#2c8bf45a4025

[21] Ariane Hegewisch and Adiam Tesfaselassie, "Fact Sheet: The Gender Wage Gap by Occupation 2018 and by Race

women in these occupations, a variety of challenges present themselves for those women who work with mostly men.

First of which is that there is still a perpetuated belief about women's leadership abilities being inferior to that of their male counterparts. When women are authoritative and lead projects they may be recognized as having competent management skills however this may come at a risk of being seen as unlikable as they can be perceived as 'too strong' a personality. By contrast, if women ease back and decide to lead with more nurturing and communicative approaches instead of being authoritative, decisive and assertive, they could be liked more but their leadership skills are questioned. So often women are seen either as likeable or as competent - not both. This is often referred to as the double-bind dilemma. [22]

Another pervasive stereotype that is held particularly close to the chest of male-dominated industries is the view of women as mothers or as office housekeepers. This derives from the constant competition for masculinity in industries dominated by men. In 2018, it was proposed that Masculinity Contest Cultures (MCCs) were the source of "dysfunctional organizational climates (e.g., rife with toxic leadership,

---

and Ethnicity" Institute for Women's Policy Research, April 2, 2019.

[22] "Infographic: The Double-Bind Dilemma for Women in Leadership," Catalyst, August 2, 2018, https://www.catalyst.org/research/infographic-the-double-bind-dilemma-for-women-in-leadership/

bullying, harassment) associated with poor individual outcomes for men as well as women (e.g., burnout, low organizational dedication, lower well-being)." [23] (Berdahl et al, 2018) But for many women in leadership who are already working in these industries they must compete and play to survive.

In industries such as law and engineering, women and people of color are expected to play a supporting role and they are expected to not compete in the in-group MCCs that drive the company culture. Women of all races report higher rates of "office housework." Both women and all people of color report feeling the pressure to sit back and let others lead, and that they should accept and are given less prestigious work. Key weapons in the masculinity contests are self-promotion, anger and assertiveness, yet when women and people of color utilize these weapons to their advantage, they are more likely than white men to report pushback from leadership and colleagues.

Therefore, it is an inherent risk for women to step out of the "housekeeper" stereotype and participate in these masculinity contests despite the fact that these behaviours and competitions can drive the entirety of a company's culture and become the way that work gets done. [24]

---

[23] Jennifer L. Berdahl et al, "Work as a Masculinity Contest," *Social Issues 74*, no. 3 (2018): 442-448 https://doi.org/10.1111/josi.12289

[24] Berdahl, "Work as a Masculinity Contest," 443.

In addition to higher stress and lack of mentoring for women in male-dominated industries, perhaps one of the most serious and arduous barriers that women experience in these occupations is sexual harassment. In male-dominated industries, reports of sexual harassment are higher. In fact, 28% of women stated that they had personally experienced sexual harassment working in a male-dominated industry. [25] This problem exists before women are able to enter the industry as women experience more harassment when pursuing their degrees at universities dominated by males comparatively to other degrees. [26] This is a constant indignance for women who are interested in fields like STEM, engineering, law, or even creative fields like video game design. Women are climbing an uphill battle in industries and universities that are predominantly male. They are actively trying to find a balance between taking charge and taking care, avoiding the white male competition while working to be seen as more than a housekeeper, and still dealing with rampant sexual harassment.

What Can You Do?

[25] Kim Parker, "Women in Majority-Male Workplaces Report Higher Rates of Gender Discrimination," Pew Research Center, March 7, 2018, https://www.pewresearch.org/fact-tank/2018/03/07/women-in-majority-male-workplaces-report-higher-rates-of-gender-discrimination/

[26] Dilshani Sarathchandra et al., "It's Broader than Just My Work Here": Gender Variations in Accounts of Success among Engineers in U.S. Academia," *Social Sciences 7*, no. 3 (2018): 32, https://doi.org/10.3390/socsci7030032

So, is it just lose-lose-lose? With all of these barriers and challenges, women may be turned off from even entering a male-dominated industry in the first place. But no matter what type of industry women are in, no matter your gender or the corporate culture, you can always take steps to improve and thrive in your own workplace by building your skills and implementing actionable strategies to pull through and place yourself on top. Here are 2 more tools to unpack and help you get there:

Three Key Ways to Overcome the "Double-Bind" Dilemma

So, women can take charge or take care but not both without either being seen as incompetent or being disliked. This is why is called the 'double-bind' dilemma. The following are strategies for dismantling this dilemma that faces women in leadership.

- **Call out Bias** - If you notice it, say something. If your colleagues and employees are perpetuating a negative stereotype, it's important that as a leader you take the steps to speak out and shut this type of behavior down at the time it is happening. Don't be undermined by phrases like "she's so emotional" and "she talks too much."

- **Be Unbiased** - When evaluating employees, apply the same standard to yourself - Ensure that you are using the same language no matter an employee's gender. Imagine the employee that you're reviewing is the opposite sex; does this affect your assessment? It shouldn't.

- **Be a Champion** - Set the stage for other women. Celebrate each other's accomplishments, advocate for professional development, and pave the way for more women in leadership by being an active, positive role model. [27]

Be Your Own Advocate: Six Ways to Excel in a Male-Dominated Workplace

When everything is working against you, you must be your own advocate. The following are strategies outlined by Jane Fang, a Harvard graduate and investment banking analyst. Her time working in finance and in sports has allowed her to gain and share several methods of overcoming an old boys club.

1. **Vocalize** - you are not going to get that project that you want or nix that new product if you do not speak up. Chances are your male colleagues have no problem vocalizing their opinions, concerns and exactly what they want. A good way to let opportunities and projects pass you by is to say nothing at all. Grab your boss in the hallway or schedule some time to meet with him or her to ensure that you are not getting left in the dark and in silence.

---

[27] Catalyst, "Infographic: The Double-Bind Dilemma for Women in Leadership."

2. **"Beer is for Bonding"**[28] - As discussed earlier, networking and finding support can be one of the most important aspects of navigating a male-dominated industry. So, if your colleagues ask you for a beer, you should make your best-effort to spend that time outside of work bonding and networking. If you're being shunned or purposefully not invited, try organizing your own happy hour, inviting those that are going to be in your corner and that you can build relationships with.

3. **Emotional Intelligence** - This skill of regulating your emotions as a woman in leadership when the gender ratio is not in your favor is of the utmost importance. Call out gender bias and negative stereotypes but pick your battles. In order to develop relationships and networks in a male-dominated industry, you may need to work on this balance of emotional regulation while also ensuring that you are still an advocate for other women leaders.

4. **Don't be the Housekeeper** - To avoid falling into the trap of the "housekeeper" stereotype, ensure that you set a standard from the moment you enter your position. You are not an assistant. You are not a coffee-getter. If your male peers are not doing this

---

[28] Jane Fang, "7 Ways to Excel in a Male-Dominated Workplace," The Muse, accessed October 28, 2020, https://www.themuse.com/advice/7-ways-to-excel-in-a-maledominated-workplace

for you or for your boss, you should certainly not be doing it for your boss.

5. **Say No** - Women in male-dominated industries may feel that they need to prove themselves to their colleagues which may involve taking on a variety of projects at all times, saying "yes" to everything. "If you never say no, you'll ultimately just hurt both yourself and your company." (Fang, N.D.)[29] Pick out projects that you're passionate about and that you truly want.

6. **"Play to your Strengths"**[30] - If you're a highly emotional-intelligent leader, show that and use it. Even though your colleagues may approach you to help them with empathy or feelings because you're a woman, you don't need to turn them away from this stereotype if it something that you are actually proficient at. Advocate for the qualities and traits that make you an effective leader.

Entrepreneurs

After considering the traditional corporate setting and male-dominated industries, it is important to consider some alternative contexts and their challenges that women in leadership may face such as women in entrepreneurship as well as strategies that

---

[29] Fang, "7 Ways to Excel in a Male-Dominated Workplace."

[30] Fang, "7 Ways to Excel in a Male-Dominated Workplace."

entrepreneurial women can use to overcome these barriers.

Though women-owned businesses are still in the minority, as of 2017 more than 11 million businesses in the US were owned by women with 5.4 million of those being majority-owned by women of color. [31] However, as in most challenges that women in leadership encounter, defying societal expectations and norms may be the first and most predominant of the barriers that women entrepreneurs deal with. For example, walking into a networking event or a business conference for entrepreneurs, women will likely encounter male-dominated rooms. In this situation, it may be easy to fall into the competition seen in a traditional masculine workplace, matching whichever stereotypical attitude is adopted by the surrounding entrepreneurs.

Successful women in leadership will find their own voice as this is the key to breaking through the societal expectations that envelop them. You must have confidence in who you are as an individual, as a woman and as an entrepreneur. Hilary Genga, founder and CEO of Trunkettes said,

> "Don't conform yourself to a man's idea of what a leader should look like."

---

[31] "Women Business Owner Statistics," NAWBO, 2019, https://www.nawbo.org/resources/women-business-owner-statistics

Take the steps to set yourself apart by showing the qualities and elements of your leadership with confidence and tenacity and that room in that networking event full of men suddenly doubles in size.

A secondary challenge for women entrepreneurs is gaining access to funds and capital. Those who need investors to help get their businesses off the ground know that the pitching process is a grueling one and for women even more so. A Babson College Report that was published in 2014 reported that less than 3% of venture capital funded companies had CEOs that were women. However, they also found that venture capitalists play to what they know - firms with women partners are more than twice as likely to invest if the executive team consists of other women. Further, if the CEO was a woman, the women venture capital partners are more than three times as likely to invest. [32] In order for these networks to develop and flourish, however, more women need to take on partner positions at venture capital firms.

Since 1999, the number of women partners has dropped from 10% to 6%,[33] a concerning drop when the workplace is meant to be modernizing and becoming more accessible for women in leadership. Women should look to building an effective plan and a

---

[32] Michael Chmura, "Venture Capital Funding Women Entrepreneurs Study," Babson College, September 30, 2014, https://www.babson.edu/about/news-events/babson-announcements/venture-capital-funding-women-entrepreneurs-study/

[33] Chmura, "Venture Capital Funding Women Entrepreneurs Study."

good team behind them no matter the gender of the partners that they will be pitching to. It's important for you to consider possible connections that will be advantageous. For example, if you are a graduate of Yale, you may want to look for investors who are also alumni. It's rare that women are able to use their gender to their advantage in the field of business but companies like Hera Hub, a coworking space for entrepreneurial women, are looking to invest in women-led businesses as well as to inspire and encourage, and to grow and support. So, be strategic about your use of connections that will grow your business. Women entrepreneurs can also raise necessary capital by asking for exactly what they need and proving the success of their business through valuation. Ensure that you've proven that your valuation can grow. If you have an expert team that is able to operate your business efficiently and prove your growth, then investors will have confidence in you and your team.

Another challenge that women entrepreneurs may encounter as well as women in general is the unintentional minimizing of their own accomplishments. Young girls are brought up and encouraged to be communal and to build consensus. Young girls are not meant to boast or convey their own value. So, when women enter leadership positions and specifically entrepreneurship, they may run into a constant barrier of feeling like they should downplay their value in order to make their colleagues and clients feel more comfortable. Own what you've accomplished. Do not feel afraid to use the word "I" when speaking to your achievements. The founder of Virtual Work Team, Shilonda Downing, put it this way,

"I've had to catch myself on occasion
when I noticed that I'm giving away
too much without a financial
commitment from a potential client.
[I] recommend other women value
their knowledge as well."

Overcoming this particular challenge comes mostly from confidence. You may know that you have the knowledge and skills to accomplish a task or a project, but you must convey this to potential clients and your colleagues. When speaking to women in leadership and in entrepreneurship, this confidence can also come from preparation. Backup your case and pitch with prepared statistics and facts. Brainstorm beforehand what questions may be asked and formulate your answers in advance so that you are not caught off guard. This can help you avoid another challenge that women in these situations sometimes encounter: the struggle to be taken seriously. Confidence is the key when earning respect in male-dominated industries and within the process of building your own business. This will assist with building up your reputation within your industry and with potential investors. But ensure that the way you perceive yourself does not fall by the wayside.

Negative self-talk is the enemy of confidence.

Women notoriously speak negatively about themselves, their bodies and their qualities. A KPMG Women's Leadership study found that 67% of women felt that they needed more support to build confidence as leaders.[34] Companies like WANT (Women Against Negative Talk) are working to change this perpetual cycle of low-confidence and constant mental negativity. Negative talk has become so normal for women that WANT views it as a "safe zone of stagnation." It prevents us from making lasting changes and from finding true solutions. [35]

Here are some actionable strategies you can use to combat negative self-talk:

- **Pay attention** - Notice and become aware of when you're being self-critical.

- **Set limitations** - negative self-talk may be unavoidable for some of us, but you can contain it. Set a time where you will allow yourself to be negative or allow your inner critic to only make comments on certain aspects of your life.

- **Consider your perception** - Consider that your thoughts and feelings do not always reflect reality. It likely is not accurate in any way to how you are seen by others.

---

[34]"KPMG Women's Leadership Study: Moving Women Forward into Leadership Roles," *KPMG International*, 2015, https://assets.kpmg/content/dam/kpmg/ph/pdf/ThoughtLeade rshipPublications/KPMGWomensLeadershipStudy.pdf

[35] "The WANT Manifesto," WANT: Women Against Negative Talk, July 12, 2020, https://womenagainstnegativetalk.com/manifesto/

- **Label your inner-critic** - Give her a name. Think of her as a force outside of yourself; therefore, making it easier to disagree with her and making her less threatening.

- **"Change negativity to neutrality"**[36]- Adjust the intensity of language that you are using against yourself. Change "I hate…" to "I don't like…" or even "I'd rather do…" Starting to use more gentle language will ease the power of your negative self-talk.

- **Would you say it to a friend?** - Speak to yourself as you would your own friends, colleagues or children. If you would not be cruel and belittling to them, do not do it to yourself.

Another challenge that women entrepreneurs may encounter is building a network to support themselves. This is already difficult in a corporate environment and in male-dominated industries, but it is especially difficult when you are working, potentially, with a smaller group of colleagues. According to Inc, almost half of all female founders declare that a lack of accessible mentors and advisors has held them back in their careers and from developing professionally. [37]

---

[36] Elizabeth Scott, "How to Reduce Negative Self-Talk for a Better Life," Verywell Mind, February 25, 2020, https://www.verywellmind.com/negative-self-talk-and-how-it-affects-us-4161304

[37] Lisa Calhoun, "30 Surprising Facts About Female Founders," Inc.com, July 6, 2015, https://www.inc.com/lisa-calhoun/30-surprising-facts-about-female-founders.html

For entrepreneurs, it's absolutely critical to have a stable support network but it can be difficult to facilitate introductions and connections and breakthrough into the high-level business world when it is still so dominated by men. In order to find a women-focused support network, you may want to try networking events that are catered towards women in business like the WIN Conference and Bizwomen events. There are also multiple online groups and forums that are created for women entrepreneurs like Ellevate Network and EveryWoman.

Once you have gathered a network that you feel confident in and supported by, it's time to ask for what you need. Kathleen Tierney, the Executive Vice President and Chief Operating Office of Chubb Insurance, said,

> Leaders need... the ability to ask really good questions even when they don't always have all the answers. Great leaders are able to see trends that others can't, to see the big picture, to ask the pointed questions, to set the goal and get people to that common goal, and to celebrate successes or quickly rethink and retool.[38]

---

[38] Laura Katen, "6 High-Powered Women Share Their Secrets for Success," The Muse, June 19, 2020, https://www.themuse.com/advice/6-highpowered-women-share-their-secrets-for-success

Utilize your support network to assist with those questions that you may not have the answer to. Most importantly, don't be afraid to ask them in the first place. Asking questions is not a sign of weakness but of strength and competence.

Laura K. Inamedinova is the innovator and founder of LKI Consulting. She is an entrepreneur who has secured contracts with several billion-dollar companies by overcoming the barriers of entrepreneurship and not accepting that gender plays a role in her business's success. She argues that,

> What does play instead are
> personality traits and attitude
> towards business, and overcoming
> the inner barriers that hold women
> back from making it big. Young
> women should accept their fears and
> push fiercely towards their goals.
> Yes, it's going to be hard. You will feel
> stressed and anxious, but just keep
> going.[39]

Creative and Cultural Industries

Another workplace setting in which women experience persistent challenges and barriers is within creative and cultural industries (CCI). There are several factors

---

[39] Simonetta Lein, "10 Inspiring Women Entrepreneurs on Overcoming Self-Doubt and Launching Your Dream," *Entrepreneur*, July 13, 2020, https://www.entrepreneur.com/article/352948

that have led to gaps in employment opportunities, wages and perception in these industries that affect women leaders on a regular basis.

The British Council completed a study in 2018 related to gender equality and empowerment in these industries and found that there is a visible gender difference between creative industries that are considered more business-related versus the cultural-related sectors. The male dominated sectors include commercial filmmaking, performing arts, architecture IT and TV while libraries, museums, publishing and documentary photo and video predominantly include more women. However, in all sub-sectors, leadership positions were mostly filled by men. It was also found that these leadership positions were perceived as "decent work" and received more support from society and the public for men while for women their creative jobs were considered more of a temporary hobby in which they are simply having fun rather than being taken seriously as a career. Interestingly enough, the respondents in the British Council study did not believe that a person's sex affected them being a good leader. However, there is a clear difference between the way these leaders are perceived which is further proven by behavioral patterns.

There is an unspoken hierarchy of business industries. A majority of the time, creative industries are not as highly regarded as financial or market-based industries. This problem is incrementally worse for women. Women often undervalue their work more and accept jobs that pay less because they may be seen as "less competitive" in the market due to societal perception of eventual maternity leave and ingrained questioning of women's professionalism especially in fields that are technology related. This can also be a barrier for men and it can affect both genders negatively. Even in modern times, men feel more pressure to be "the breadwinner" so they are drawn more to jobs that are less creative but with higher pay. Even in sectors that are viewed as highly "feminized" such as fashion design, gay men are more likely to hold senior positions, receive better pay and are recognized more for their achievements than women. [40]

These challenges and gender biases must be addressed in the creative and cultural industries as they are perhaps one of the most efficient tools to promote gender equality and to break down held stereotypes that affect women leaders. In media, in public spaces and events, there is a multitude of content created by CCI artists and professionals; therefore, the messages generated by those creatives can directly influence awareness of gender issues and barriers in society. As the British Council states:

> Strengthening CCI as a sector of the economy that provides decent jobs, sustainable working environment, formalization of the economies, e-commerce growth, increasing markets' sophistication, all factors seen across the region, are supportive trends for professionalization of the sector and

---

[40] Colette Henry, "Women and the Creative Industries: Exploring the Popular Appeal," *Creative Industries Journal 2*, no. 2 (2009): 143-160, 10.1386/cij.2.2.143/1

gender empowerment within CCI and
through CCI.[41]

So, women in leadership should take the steps in the creative industry to support gender empowerment. Even those not in creative fields should do their best to encourage and bolster women in creative positions to help in the fight against these gender barriers that society still holds.

Speaking Out Against Gender Bias/Harassment

It may seem idyllic and near terrifying to speak out against barriers and bias that are specific to gender. No matter what industry you work in, as a woman in leadership, you are likely to experience some sort of bias or harassment at some point in your career. Statistically, 3 out 4 (77%) women will experience verbal forms of sexual harassment comparatively to 34% of men. 38% of women reported that they experienced sexual harassment within their workplace. [42] Further to this, women in leadership

---

[41]"Gender Equality and Empowerment in the Creative and Cultural Industries," *British Council*, 2018, https://www.britishcouncil.org/sites/default/files/gender_equality_and_empowerment_cci_eastern_partnership_2018_en-compressed.pdf

[42] "2018 Study on Sexual Harassment and Assault," Stop Street Harassment, February 21, 2018, http://www.stopstreetharassment.org/our-work/nationalstudy/2018-national-sexual-abuse-report/.

compared to women who aren't are more likely to experience sexual harassment.

The Swedish Institute for Social Research completed a study where they surveyed women in the United States, Sweden and Japan, and they found that not only are women leaders more likely to be harassed but that the highest incidences of harassment were found in the US. The American women leaders had between a 50% to 100% likelihood of experiencing harassment. This was attributed by the researchers to the fact that women in leadership positions, especially middle management, are susceptible and exposed to harassment from two potential perpetrators-subordinates and higher-level management. [43]

Though women may be encouraged by close friends and family and the leaders at companies to speak out against these harassments and biases, most women do not because of a few different factors but perhaps the most common and demoralizing is backlash.

Employees seem generally reluctant to report harassment as they fear that it will hurt their careers. According to a 2017 survey. [44] Jill Katz, the CEO and founder of Assemble HR states,

---

[43] Olle Folke et al., "Sexual Harassment of Women Leaders," *Daedalus 149*, no. 1 (2020): 180-197, https://doi.org/10.1162/daed_a_01781

[44] Elizabeth Franks, "Sexual Harassment in the Workplace," MEAA, January 29, 2018, https://www.meaa.org/news/sexual-harassment-in-the-workplace/.

Some people worry there may be
great risks in raising an issue
because once you've officially spoken
up, there's no turning back.
Unfortunately, to some, the risks may
feel so serious that they choose to
keep quiet.[45]

In recent years, there has been retaliation towards women speaking up about their experiences in the MeToo movement. A woman who stands up and raises her hand to report a bias or a stereotype within her industry is often pegged as a nuisance, a whistleblower, or a troublemaker. This type of retaliation perpetuates the notion that it is safer for women to keep quiet about harassment.

Women who have accomplished the move into leadership positions are often subject to more harassment. Coming back to the Swedish Institute for Social Research study, additional data suggested that women who've advanced their careers are also more likely to gain the reputation as "trouble maker" due to negative professional and social consequences related to speaking out. [46] The risks are higher. A woman in leadership who has broken through the glass ceiling

---

[45] Cate Luzio, "MeToo's Next Frontier: Addressing Backlash After Speaking Up," Forbes (Forbes Magazine, April 29, 2019),
https://www.forbes.com/sites/cateluzio/2019/04/28/metoos-next-frontier-addressing-backlash-after-speaking-up/.

[46]Olle Folke et al., "Sexual Harassment of Women Leaders," 190

has farther to fall. So, women stay silent to avoid risking their reputation and being seen as a victim.

Despite the fact that 98% of organizations have sexual harassment workplace policies, [47] women are still experiencing harassment. According to the US Equal Employment Opportunity Commission (EEOC) 75% of victims of harassment experienced retaliation when they decided to speak up. This is an indicator that the backlash from speaking out has become a major deterrent for women to tell the truth of their experiences. The EEOC goes further and reports:

> Unwanted physical touching was formally reported only 8% of the time; and sexually coercive behavior was reported by only 30% of the women who experienced it. ... Studies have found that 6% to 13% of individuals who experience harassment file a formal complaint. That means that, on average, anywhere from 87% to 94% of individuals did not file a formal complaint.[48]

---

[47] University of Missouri-Columbia, "Gender perceptions of sexual harassment can influence workplace policy effectiveness: Organizations could benefit from sexual harassment training that acknowledges the gender dynamics of harassment," ScienceDaily, accessed October 30, 2020, www.sciencedaily.com/releases/2016/04/160407155557.htm

[48] Chai R Feldman and Victoria A Lipnic, "Select Task Force on the Study of Harassment in the Workplace," U.S. Equal Employment Opportunity Commission, June 2016,

The EEOC advises that there is some improvement in training specifically related to bystander training and providing workplace-specific development. [49]But the first line of defence may lie in your own hands. Those in middle-management are present during the day-to-day operations, the leaders that employees see every day - they set the precedent for acceptable versus unacceptable behavior. Any shift in company culture should stem from top-level executives however middle managers are the ones who implement and spot and address problems. So, if you do not yet have the tools to handle sexual harassment when an employee confides in you, it is important to seek professional development. Here are 13 actionable strategies that you can follow as a comprehensive plan if an employee approaches you:

1. **Policy First:** Ensure that your organization's sexual harassment policy is posted and that all of your employees are aware of it. Advocate and ensure that it is understood that sexual harassment will be investigated and punished and that it will not be tolerated at your workplace.

2. **More than One Way:** Employee's should have multiple options when they decide to make a formal complaint. Human Resources is an excellent option to take complaints; however, it may also fall on your shoulders as the manager or

---

https://www.eeoc.gov/select-task-force-study-harassment-workplace.

[49] Feldman and Lipnic, "Select Task Force on the Study of Harassment in the Workplace."

supervisor. Others in leadership positions may also be a good option if they are not involved.

3. **Take it Seriously:** Whether the complaint is made formally with a report or informally over lunch, it should be taken seriously. It is not always clear whether an employee is officially reporting harassment or simply 'venting,' but no matter the level of complaint, the same procedure should be followed according to your company's policy.

4. **Guarantee Safety:** Advise the employee who has filed the complaint that they are safe from retaliation and take the steps to implement their protection. This may mean removing the alleged harasser from their current location in the workplace. The employee should advise you of any possible retaliation or ongoing harassment immediately.

5. **Avoid Gaslighting:** Reassure the employee that they made the right decision to report the harassment. Ask questions to get the full story, but do not question the employee's integrity or validity. Take notes and listen carefully as they tell you what happened. Ensure your notes are thorough and detailed.

6. **Next Steps:** Inform both of the parties of the next steps that you and the company will take to move forward.

7. **Investigate and Interview:** Perform a thorough and unbiased investigation. Interview in the same manner as you did the complainant. Ask open-

ended questions and take thorough notes. Start first with any potential witnesses to seek facts followed by interviewing the person who is accused. Do your best to maintain the same respectful approach and avoid gaslighting.

8. **Reach a Conclusion:** After completing the investigation and you've reviewed the notes and the facts, you must come to an unbiased conclusion based on what you've uncovered. You may need to discuss the case with others in leadership and Human Resources. The conclusion should include the next steps whether it be termination, training or that no harassment occurred.

9. **Communicate the Conclusion:** Inform both parties of the determination and the next steps that will be taken to resolve the issue. For the safety of both the accuser and the accused, this information should be kept on a very 'need-to-know basis.'[50]

10. **Discipline:** After determining and communicating the conclusion, the discipline step may not be an easy one. It may involve giving the harasser a notice of termination or sending them for mandatory training.

---

[50] Erik J. Martin, "How to Handle a Sexual Harassment Complaint," U.S. Chamber of Commerce, March 20, 2019, https://www.uschamber.com/co/run/human-resources/how-to-deal-with-sexual-harassment-complaint

11. **Follow Up:** Whether harassment was determined or not, follow up with both the complainant and the accused with documentation. Follow up regularly with the complainant to make sure that he or she is comfortable at work and that there is no continuation of harassment.

12. **Accept Imperfection:** No investigation is perfect. You may have issues corroborating the employee's story if there are no witnesses. Ask for help if you need it. Speak with an attorney. Do your best with what information you have.

13. **Take Care:** The reporting of sexual harassment and completing an investigation will be stressful process on the complainant, the accused, on HR and on yourself as a woman in leadership. Do not forget to take care of yourself during this process as well with stress management techniques and getting proper nourishment and sleep. [51]

Liane Tessier, a firefighter in Nova Scotia, Canada, provides a candid view on her experience with reporting gender bias and sexual harassment in a male-dominated industry. Not only was she subjected to discrimination and harassment throughout her career as a firefighter but when she decided to speak up in 2005 she was "ignored and dismissed" by those that she reached out to for help and this included

---

[51] Susan M Heathfield, "How to Handle an Employee Sexual Harassment Complaint," The Balance Careers, July 13, 2020, https://www.thebalancecareers.com/how-to-address-an-employee-sexual-harassment-complaint-1916862

government agencies. [52] She was labelled as the "troublemaker" and as "crazy" and even her other female colleagues avoided her, not willing to speak of their own experiences or even Liane's. There was no support. Even if the agencies were willing to help, at that time they were ill-equipped, not knowing how to handle this problem that affects millions of women.

Tessier also worked as a stevedore at the docks, unloading and loading cargo, where she, again, experienced harassment in a male-dominated industry. She was verbally assaulted on more than one occasion with the breaking point culminating to an incident in the lunchroom when one of the men told her to "shut the F up, you hairy-legged whore!" At this point, she already had a human rights case resting with the city about her experiences as a firefighter, so she had to make a difficult but crucial decision: speak out again or stay silent. Both options would come with consequences that Tessier knew too well. When she returned to work, not only had the incident spread through the docks, rampant with misinformation of what actually happened, but she had also been labelled as "crazed, violent and unstable" by her male coworkers. [53] In addition, the president of the union suggested that she was at least partly to blame for the harassment because of the way she handled it. Tessier was livid. She filed a formal complaint. She spoke out.

---

[52] Liane Tessier, "Why Women Don't Speak Out," Guts Magazine," April 29, 2015, http://gutsmagazine.ca/why-women-dont-speak-out/

[53] Tessier, "Why Women Don't Speak Out," Guts Magazine."

Tessier received backlash from her coworkers with no support from the union and employers that still continues to this day. They ignored her, criticized her and alienated her. And this was not the only backlash Tessier had to deal with; she was also subjected to cyber bullying. She again submitted a complaint, and in total seriousness, the employer and the union advised her that if she wanted this backlash and persecution to stop, she needed to stop filing complaints. Tessier attributes some of this victim blaming and the impetus to stay silent on the pure inability and cluelessness of organizational leaders when it comes to sexual harassment complaints. She states:

> This systemic inattention feeds into our fears and leads us to silence that perpetuates the ongoing discrimination that continues to plague us. Systemic discrimination, however, is dependent on our silence around harassment. The men who perpetuate this system know this, and continue to hope that women will continue to be complacent and silent, too afraid to speak up.[54]

In November 2013, the Supreme Court of Nova Scotia finally ordered a re-examination of Tessier's gender discrimination complaint that was filed back in 2007. After years of fighting against discrimination and gender bias, mostly alone, Tessier would be entitled to a new investigation. She recognizes that there never should have been such a struggle to begin with and, of

---

[54] Tessier, "Why Women Don't Speak Out," Guts Magazine."

course, that much of these issues lie with systematic stereotypes that drive the economy and society. However, Tessier also challenges other women to be leaders against harassment after speaking with female colleagues that advised that they would never feel safe speaking out and filing complaints.

> ...I wasn't born in a vacuum separate from other women, and neither were they. We are all in this together, whether getting harassed or standing up for ourselves. I am a product of my mother, who in turn was a product of her mother, and we are all allies in the struggle against harassment and discrimination.

Yes, the consequences of speaking out are severe, terrifying, and potentially isolating. But for those of us that can, especially women in leadership who are able to speak out, you must find the courage to do so.

> Ultimately, silence results in a society which is naïve to the realities of gender-based violence towards all women. By speaking up, we show how difficult the fight still is for women, and how far we still have to go. By speaking up, we can spread awareness to the public and we can change the way workplace discrimination is understood and handled in public media. [55]

---

[55] Tessier, "Why Women Don't Speak Out," Guts Magazine."

Tessier is a shining example of a woman speaking out against harassment and gender bias despite the surrounding relentless challenges that she had to face. As women in leadership, you can begin to pave the path for systematic change through your responses to complaints, your management of male-dominated industries and by your own confidence and courage as entrepreneurs and trailblazers.

Chapter 3: NAVIGATE: How To Thrive at Different Stages in Your Career

Overview

It is clear that women experience different challenges based on their workplace setting. Whether it be a male-dominated industry, traditional corporate setting, entrepreneurship or a creative industry, women in leadership experience a variety of challenges related to gender disparity, roles and stereotypes. Therefore, you should consider where you are in your journey as a female leader. What are the barriers and challenges that you have experienced in different stages of life? Young leaders may have different barriers than those re-entering the workforce or mature leaders. Furthermore, mothers who are managers at work often have to deal with the massive challenge of balancing business and family life. Let's address these stages and their testing of leadership one by one.

Young Women in Leadership

Being young and ambitious usually has many advantages. It can lead to early promotions and establishing your career before some of your friends have even graduated from college. However, entering leadership as a young woman can also have many impediments that affect not only our perception of the work world but of ourselves.

The first challenge young women leaders may experience is "the likability factor." [56] And this may come back to the Double-Bind Dilemma as discussed earlier that it is inherently more difficult for women to be seen as both competent and liked at the same time. Though being assertive and direct may have gotten you to your position in the first place, when you are placed into managerial positions it can become a direct contradiction to what society believes women leaders should be. Anytime a woman spearheads a contradiction of societal perceptions, it is met with negative reactions. Take Greta Thunberg, for example, the Swedish environmental activist who paved the way for Gen Z leadership and a surge of protests related to climate change. She is known for being straight-forward and direct and her speeches have been met with a resounding amount of criticism, backlash, and animosity. Not only because of her views, but because she is directly challenging the perception of what we expect from a girl of her age. Chris Kenny of Sky News Australia described her as a "hysterical teenager" who needs to be cared for.[57] She's also been described as

[56] Ciera Graham, "Barriers and Biases: 4 Challenges Faced by Millennial Women Leaders," The Seattle Times (The Seattle Times Company, February 20, 2020), https://www.seattletimes.com/explore/careers/barriers-and-biases-4-challenges-faced-by-millennial-women-leaders/

[57]Sky News Australia. "The UN is 'taking advantage of hysterical teen' Greta Thunberg." YouTube video, 4:57, September 23, 2019. https://youtu.be/UDXKTXuM2TY

"mentally-ill,"[58] "unstable,"[59] and a "millenarian weirdo."[60] One even claimed that Thunberg needed a "spanking."[61] Her ideas have become a tertiary factor in the list of reasons why she has been met with so much resistance.

So, as a young woman in leadership, there is no doubt that you may have more of a challenge gaining buy-in from older colleagues and they may even question your authority. Perhaps not even because of your ideas or strategies but simply because you have defied an inherent societal perception.

A second challenge that young women leaders may experience is the pressure of the expectations that are

---

[58] Adam Gabbatt, "Fox News Apologises to Greta Thunberg for Pundit's 'Disgraceful' Remark," The Guardian (Guardian News and Media, September 24, 2019), https://www.theguardian.com/media/2019/sep/24/fox-news-greta-thunberg-michael-knowles

[59] Aletha Adu, "Piers and Susanna Row as He Calls Activist Greta Thunberg 'Unstable'," The Sun (The Sun, October 11, 2019), https://www.thesun.co.uk/news/10002266/greta-thunberg-piers-morgan-criticise-unstable-gmb/

[60] Brendan O'Neill, "The Cult of Greta Thunberg," spiked The cult of Greta Thunberg Comments (spiked, May 6, 2019), https://www.spiked-online.com/2019/04/22/the-cult-of-greta-thunberg/

[61] NolteNC. "I can't tell if Greta needs a spanking or a psychological intervention...Probably both." September 23, 2019, 12:22pm. https://twitter.com/NolteNC/status/1176185011776761857

set on them. Young women in management may feel more pressure to take on more work for fear of being perceived as lazy or incompetent. According to the Society for Industrial and Organizational Psychology, it is more difficult for women to say no when asked to help with extra work. [62] In addition to this, Manpower Group determined in 2016 that 73% of millennials work more than 40 hours a week while almost a quarter work more than 50 hours a week. [63] With these amounts of work hours, it can impact the sense of young leaders' sense of work/life balance. There are assumptions that since millennials have been delaying childbirth and marriage that they have more free time therefore more time to spend on work. [64] Therefore, when these factors are combined: difficulties saying no, limited work/life balance and pressure to take on extra work, young women in leadership may have difficulty meeting the expectations of their leaders and the

---

[62] Clif Boutelle, "What Is I-O?," SIOP News, March 12, 2014, http://old.siop.org/article_view.aspx?article=1336

[63]"Millenial Careers: 2020 Vision. Facts, Figures and Practical Advice from Workforce Experts," *Manpower Group,* 2016. Wisconsin: Manpower Group. https://www.manpowergroup.com/wps/wcm/connect/660ebf65-144c-489e-975c-9f838294c237/MillennialsPaper1_2020Vision_lo.pdf?MOD=AJPERES

[64] Hillary Hoffower, "The US Birthrate Is the Lowest It's Been in 32 Years, and It's Partly Because Millennials Can't Afford Having Kids," Business Insider (Business Insider, May 24, 2019), https://www.businessinsider.com/us-birthrate-decline-millennials-delay-having-kids-2019-5

colleagues around them. This pressure is likely magnified based on the level of management.

A third more and complicated challenge that young women leaders may experience is "the experience conundrum."[65] Especially in highly competitive workforces, young people tend to have high levels of education and this is increasing over time. According to a Pew Research Center analysis of Current Population, they found that almost half (46%) of women ages 25 to 29 had a bachelor's degree or more in 2016. This is up substantially, a 10% jump, from the year 2000 when Gen X women workers were of the same age.[66]

In the United States, the overall percent of young people employed with an education of a bachelor's degree or more was 40% in 2016 (millennials), 32% in 2000 (gen Xers), for boomers it was 26% in 1985, and finally, for the silent generation in 1964 it was 16%. Also, it's important to note, nearly 60% of bachelor's and master's degrees as of 2017 are granted to women. [67]

---

[65] Graham, "Barriers and Biases: 4 Challenges Faced by Millennial Women Leaders."

[66] Nikki Graf, "More Young Workers than Ever Are College Grads in U.S.," Pew Research Center (Pew Research Center, July 27, 2020), https://www.pewresearch.org/fact-tank/2017/05/16/todays-young-workers-are-more-likely-than-ever-to-have-a-bachelors-degree/.

[67] "Degrees Conferred by Postsecondary Institutions, by Level of Degree and Sex of Student: Selected Years, 1869-70 through 2027-28," Digest of Education Statistics, accessed November 1st, 2020.

With young people being more educated than ever, it is leaving less and less time for them to gain relevant work experience. You may have spent your early twenties going to school and earning your credentials and perhaps, you had a part-time job or a job to cover the bills, but when moving out of school, you may find that you are lacking in the necessary experience to get the job of your dreams and enter the career path that you desire. This may feel quite defeating to spend years and thousands of dollars on a graduate or undergraduate degree, only to garner an entry-level position with a low salary.

As a young woman in leadership, you may have been able to overcome this challenge by proving your skills based on merit and education rather than experience. But this challenge may arise again when you're looking to move into a higher-level position. You may be viewed as a less competitive candidate with less years of experience despite the amount of education and considerable soft skills on your resume.

According to CNBC and a New Women at Work Survey, they found that in the next 10 years 15% of women between the ages of 18-44 expected to be at a C-Suite level of management. Among the 1000 U.S. women who participated in the survey, 54% said that when it comes to their career they are "very ambitious," and 35% stated that they are "somewhat ambitious." [68]

---

https://nces.ed.gov/programs/digest/d17/tables/dt17_318.10.asp?current=yes

[68] Courtney Connley, "Ambition Is Not the Problem: Women Want the Top Jobs-They Just Don't Get Them," CNBC (CNBC, March 5, 2020),

Therefore, it seems that it is not a lack of ambition or their education that is holding back young women leaders from their goals, but perhaps this conundrum of gaining education before experience is presenting a paradoxical barrier that is becoming more and more difficult to surmount over time. More education leads to more job prospects, but more education means less time for work experience, and less work experience leads to less job prospects.

Now that three major challenges for young women in leadership have been discussed, let's address two key questions:

- First, what can you do to manage and overcome these barriers?
- Second, how can young women leaders like you be supported by fellow women in management?

- **Make yourself visible** - when taking on tasks, women are often asked to complete the tasks that are viewed as "non-promotable." [69] So as young women in leadership you should make the effort to take on tasks that will not be seen

---

https://www.cnbc.com/2020/03/05/why-women-are-locked-out-of-top-jobs-despite-having-high-ambition.html

[69] Linda Babcock, Maria P Recalde, and Lise Vesterlund, "Why Women Volunteer for Tasks That Don't Lead to Promotions," Harvard Business Review, November 22, 2019, https://hbr.org/2018/07/why-women-volunteer-for-tasks-that-dont-lead-to-promotions

as "housework" or as "invisible labor." [70] When you take on a project, try to take on the tasks that best represent your competency and your maturity as a worker. And when you've finished and you've done a job well, make it visible. Do your best to take credit for your work. Exposure is validating and putting yourself and your work at the forefront will allow your colleagues to see your capabilities as a young woman in leadership.

- **Look for Role-Models** - Find other young women who have overcome barriers and see how they've navigated the challenges of their workplaces. This, however, may be difficult because we don't see many young women in leadership that we can look to in the public eye. This is a societal issue that should be rectified with more young women on conference panels, in politics and in leadership. Look to the established women in leadership at your own company to help dispel any doubts. If possible, find role models who exemplify the success that you want for yourself and that you may share some personal experiences with. A study by the Glass Hammer and Accenture done in 2013, determined that there is a strong correlation between women with leadership goals and women with role models. Especially

---

[70] Meera Jagannathan, "How Do You Get Taken Seriously at Work as a Young Woman?," MarketWatch (MarketWatch, December 31, 2018), https://www.marketwatch.com/story/how-do-you-get-taken-seriously-at-work-as-a-young-woman-2018-07-27-9884747

those in industries that are male-dominated like the technology sector. [71]

- **Build your own Network -** Along with looking for role models, young women in leadership should also look to establish a supportive network. Try making a networking plan, looking for other people in your workplace that you want in your corner and strategies that you can use to build those relationships. This may involve scheduling daily walks around the office, going out of your way to talk in the lunch room or by the water cooler, and/or attending professional development seminars and meetings. Do your best to include both men and women in your network. Sharon Vinderine, founder of Parent Test Parent Approved (PTPA) says, "If you want men to stop and listen in the workplace, you need to exude a lot of confidence in your area of expertise...You need to play to that if you want to succeed in male networking circles."[72]

---

[71] Melissa J. Anderson, Nicki Gilmour and Mekayla Castro, *Women in Technology: Leaders of Tomorrow*, (Evolved People Media: New York, 2013), http://theglasshammer.com/wp-content/uploads/2015/03/The-Glass-Hammer-Women-in-Technology-White-Paper-Final.pdf

[72] Nancy Ripton, "Ten Simple and Effective Networking Strategies for Women," Diversity, October 10, 2019, https://diversity.rbc.com/ten-simple-and-effective-networking-strategies-for-women/

- **Confidence is Key** - when you are looking to establish a network and make your work visible, confidence is one of the key factors and skills needed for young women in leadership. Confidence can be learned. If you are currently not feeling confident, one of the most effective strategies that you can implement is simply pretending that you are. Self-perception theory states that people make conclusions about who they are based on what they observe in their own behaviour. Therefore, if you want to be seen as confident, begin imitating other confident people's behaviour and the self-perception will follow. Eventually, you'll be seen as confident by others as well. [73]

- **Engage Young Men** - In 2010, a study performed by the Pan American Health Organization looked at programs around the world that promote gender equality and health that involved young men in the process of empowering young women. It concluded with young men showing an increased acceptance of domestic work and a decreased rate of violence against women. So, women in leadership, especially young women, should look to engage the young men around them in conversations about gender biases, workplace

---

[73] Oliver Burkeman, "According To 'Self Perception Theory,' Imitating Confident People Makes You More Confident," Business Insider (Business Insider, December 6, 2012), https://www.businessinsider.com/acting-confident-makes-you-more-conficent-2012-12

harassment and gender-transformative policy change. This may come with the task of framing the focus on the broader gender justice movement to develop young men and colleagues as engaged allies. [74]

Implementing these strategies above as a young woman in leadership may not be easy. As you face persistent obstacles and barriers, you will still be expected, and you may still have the ambition to move your career forward and garner accolades as a managerial woman. Kathleen Henson Sarpy, the founder and CEO of Agency H5, advises that you should be a "sponge." She states,

> ...my main piece of advice is to listen more than you speak. Be a sponge and absorb as much information as possible from as many people as possible. Watch people's styles and the ways they conduct themselves. You'll start shaping who you want to be by observing the positive and not-so-positive behaviors of others. However, as we evolve professionally, I think that some women feel pressured to stay in this listening phase for too long— sometimes for their entire career. It's like being forced to never take the

---

[74] *Engaging Young Men in Advancing Gender Equality*, (UN Women, New York, 2018), https://promundoglobal.org/wp-content/uploads/2018/10/F-Understanding-How-to-Engage-Young-Men-in-Advancing-Gender-Equality-1.pdf

training wheels off your bike even though you know you could do the Tour de France. As women, we can't be afraid to speak up, ask questions or give input. Yes, when you're just starting a job, listen. But even then, don't hesitate to ask a question, never doubt the validity of your opinion or even worse, hide your talent.[75]

Balancing Business and Family Life

Women in leadership know that business can be demanding, taxing and time-consuming especially when in a managerial role. Family life and children share these same qualities. If you are simultaneously trying to grow your business and your family, you will likely encounter several challenges and barriers that will affect this balancing act.

So, in addition to the role that women leaders hold in their company, many of them also remain the primary caretakers in their household. [76] As time goes on, the demands of the job may become increasingly strenuous and important, possibly causing a breaking

---

[75]Lindsay Tigar, "20 Inspiring Quotes and Mentorship Advice from Female Leaders," Real Simple, March 5, 2020, https://www.realsimple.com/work-life/life-strategies/job-career/women-mentorship-quotes?slide=662d05d3-1459-4a97-b6d8-2e34b1a917cf

[76] Richard Hughes, Robert Ginnett, and Gordon Curphy, Leadership: Enhancing the Lessons of Experience (New York, New York: Mcgraw Hill Higher Education, 2014).

point where women have to choose between their family and their career. Fewer women CEOs and executives have children due to the effects it can have on their career according to Jack and Suzy Welch. [77] Further, women voluntarily leave their jobs due to decisions related to family life and 32% of women decide to step out of their roles at work after having children. It can also lead to women leaders being more hesitant to travel and take on overtime hours which can further lead to less professional development and promotion opportunities. [78] [79] [80]

These interruptions in women's careers are at least partially due to the fact that gender disparity still strongly exists when it comes to child-rearing and that it is far behind the labor force trends. Women still devote more time on average than men to childcare and housework and fewer hours to paid work. Nearly

[77] Sheila Wellington, Marcia Brumit Kropf, and Paulette R Gerkovich, "What's Holding Women Back?," Harvard Business Review, August 21, 2014, https://hbr.org/2003/06/whats-holding-women-back

[78] T Woodard, "Developing Women Leaders: It's Now a Bottom-Line Issue," Competence Women, (2007): 10-11.

[79] Sylvia Ann Hewlett, "Executive Women and the Myth of Having It All," Harvard Business Review, August 21, 2014, https://hbr.org/2002/04/executive-women-and-the-myth-of-having-it-all

[80] Denise Lyons and Connie McArthur, "Gender's unspoken role in leadership evaluations," Human Resource Planning 30, no. 3 (2005): 25-32.

half of the American workforce is now made up of women; however, according to PEW research,

> "among working parents of children younger than 18, mothers in 2013 spent an average of 14.2 hours per week on housework, compared with fathers' 8.6 hours. And mothers spent 10.7 hours per week actively engaged in child care, compared with fathers' 7.2 hours." [81]

The societal expectation is not for women to return to their traditional childminding role, however. Pew Research continued with a survey done in 2012 that 79% of Americans rejected this notion. Yet very few adult Americans believed that having a mother who works full time is the "ideal situation" for young children. In fact, less than 16% of adults believed this to be true. Interestingly enough, even among working women with children only 22% of them believed that full-time working mothers was the best situation for young children. The expectation for fathers is quite different. In the same survey, 70% of adults believed that a full-time working father was ideal for young children. While 33% stated that it would be best for women to not work at all, by comparison, only 4% said

---

[81] Kim Parker, "Women More than Men Adjust Their Careers for Family Life," Pew Research Center (Pew Research Center, August 14, 2020), https://www.pewresearch.org/fact-tank/2015/10/01/women-more-than-men-adjust-their-careers-for-family-life/

it would be best for the fathers to be the ones not working. [82]

These challenges may just get worse for women as they move into higher-level executive positions. In 2002, Sylvia Ann Hewlett of the Harvard Business Review performed a nationwide survey exploring the two-faceted lives of women in leadership. The findings were "startling" and "troubling" for Hewlett. It demonstrated clear difficulties for ambitious, professional women including the merciless demands of their careers, the gender disparity and biases, and the challenges that come with bearing children late in life. These difficulties have left many professional women, particularly in the 41-to-55 age range, childless despite the majority of them yearning for children.

In addition to the factors of the disparity between the amounts of housework that each sex completes, Hewlett also found several challenges that have influenced executive-level women and their potential to have a family. One of these is the difficulty in finding a partner as a woman in management. The former managing director of Deutsche Bank in London, Tamara Adler, expresses it this way,

"In the rarified upper reaches of
high-altitude careers where the air is
thin...men have a much easier time

---

[82] "Changing Views about Work," in *Modern Parenthood* (Pew Research Centre, March 14, 2013), https://www.pewsocialtrends.org/2013/03/14/chapter-1-changing-views-about-work/#whats-ideal-for-mothers-and-fathers-with-young-children

finding oxygen. They find oxygen in
the form of younger, less driven
women who will coddle their egos.
The hard fact is that most successful
men are not interested in acquiring
an ambitious peer as a partner."[83]

Further to this, executive women may experience additional challenges as they are expected to build up their careers at the same time that they are at the ideal child-bearing age. High-achieving women may also be putting in long hours leading to not only scarcity in partners, but a scarcity in time. [84]

The executive women from Hewlett's study have called on companies for action to rectify this situation for managers with children and for managers who wish to have children. They suggested the following: "A time bank of paid parenting leave, restructured retirement plans, unpaid career break, reduced-hour careers and alumni status for former employees."[85]

Women entrepreneurs also have many challenges when trying to balance their business and their families. For Michelle Garett, an entrepreneurial Public Relations consultant, the way that she found balance was leaving her traditional corporate job and

---

[83] Hewlett, "Executive Women and the Myth of Having It All."

[84] Hewlett, "Executive Women and the Myth of Having It All."

[85] Hewlett, "Executive Women and the Myth of Having It All."

beginning her own consulting firm prior to the birth of her first child. Garett expressed the following,

> "I knew that if I had continued
> working in the corporate world ... I
> would have had to make a lot of
> choices I didn't want to make. I do
> think the culture of work is shifting
> to allow women more flexibility,
> which is a good thing. But working
> for yourself will probably always
> allow more freedom than working
> for someone else."

However, it is not always feasible to start your own company as a solution to needing a work-life balance.

Cultivate Your Own Balance

Though companies should be addressing these disparate challenges that women face through policies, there are also tools you can use for yourself. Here are five actionable strategies that you can begin to implement to assist with gaining your own balance of both business and family life:

1. **You Know your Child Best** - Despite all the parenting books and advice from other mothers, childcare is a very personal decision and ultimately you know your child and their needs better than anyone. More important than anything, choose childcare that is best for your children in your opinion. It is also important to consider practical factors for childcare like

79

proximity to work and value. Also consider the future. What will your childcare look like in 2 to 3 years? What will your role at work look like in 2 to 3 years? It may be worthwhile to enlist childcare that will be flexible as your career and your children grow.

2. **Embrace a New Perspective** - Parenting may have changed you. It may have changed your perspective on communication, time management and prioritizing. Catherine Oliver, a senior manager in group strategy says, "There are so many positive skills you learn as a parent that add a lot of value. The trick is recognising that, having confidence in yourself and just getting on with it."[86] So you do not need to treat work life and home life as entirely separate. It is likely that at times the two will overlap and you may need to make adjustments to your daily life. Try to remember that you already contain the strong characteristics and traits of a leader at work and a leader at home, redirect and apply these assets that you have to all facets of your life. [87]

---

[86] Lottie O'Conor, "Five Steps to Balancing Work and Family," The Guardian (Guardian News and Media, October 13, 2015), https://www.theguardian.com/women-in-leadership/2015/oct/13/five-steps-to-balancing-work-and-family

[87] Joelle K Jay, "3 Ways for Women Leaders to Get Their Work-Life Balance Back in Check," Inc.com (Inc., October 25, 2016), https://www.inc.com/joelle-k-jay/balance-isnt-a-myth-3-ways-for-women-leaders-to-get-their-work-life-balance-back.html

3. **Stop Saying 'Sorry'** - When trying to accomplish balance between home and work, you may experience some stumbling blocks. You may need to take more time off or reschedule meetings or you may have difficulties managing your workload. You may have to change your routine and it may take time for your colleagues to adjust to this. So, communication is key, but apologizing is not. Do your best to explain your situation and set clear expectations for yourself and for your employees while you are managing both work and family life. According to psychological science, women do apologize more than men. [88] Consider that the balance you are trying to strike is not an offense. It should be a process of managing expectations and reinforcing these expectations through better communication.

4. **Share Home Duties** - As discussed previously, women take on more of the housework than men. [89] So, when looking into strategies to manage the balance between work and home, it is essential that you set expectations at work and at home with your partner. Attempt to set up a plan for housework and childcare with

[88] Karina Schumann and Michael Ross, "Why Women Apologize More Than Men: Gender Differences in Thresholds for Perceiving Offensive Behavior," Psychological Science 21, no. 11 (2010): 1649-55, 10.1177/0956797610384150

[89] Parker, "Women More than Men Adjust Their Careers for Family Life."

your partner that involves an equal share of work so that you are not taking on the brunt of the duties at home. Both men and women need to take the steps to lead this change in expectations around housework. Louise Webster, the founder of beyondtheschoolrun.com, says, "Men need to be as clear as mothers and speak out: they must say that they need to get home to put their children to bed; that they need to get to their children's nativity." [90] Aspire to develop a strong partnership where both you and your spouse can break through this gender disparity. If you are a single mother, look to your support network to form partnerships. Neighbors, friends, or members of a local organization or church may be able to assist with childcare while you make progress on the housework or run out to the store, or vice versa.

5. **You are Not Alone** - The transition to parenthood can be a very tough period in a working women's life. It is bound to come with stress and potential feelings of guilt and worry. Accept that these feelings are only feelings, and it is important to let them come and then let them pass. This progression in your life will not be a perfect one and striving for perfection may only lead to more anxieties. You can consider speaking with other parents and mothers about their experiences and strategies. Take the time to be honest and share how you have been

---

[90] O'Conor, "Five Steps to Balancing Work and Family."

feeling about your balance and what has and has not worked for you. You are not alone in this fight. Journalist and senior director, Anniki Sommerville expresses her own thoughts on parenthood,

"One of the things about being a parent is that you never feel like you've 'arrived' and achieved perfection. You embrace chaos and uncertainty a little more."

As women in leadership, you may be able to go further to support working mothers in your organization. Even if you are not a parent yourself if you are in a position to implement change. You may want to consider some of the strategies below outlined by Bird in 2006 [91] to better support work-life balance:

- Publicize policy change - If you are pulling together new and improved work-life benefits, procedures, and policies, ensure that you communicate this to staff. Advise them that you are working towards a change in the company to better support them.

---

[91] Jim Bird, "Work-Life balance: Doing it right and avoiding the pitfalls," *Employment Relations Today 33*, no. 3, (2006): 21, https://worklifebalance.com/app/themes/wlb/assets/pdfs/article3.pdf

- Dissolve internal meetings on Friday afternoons

- If the employee has put in considerable hours earlier in the week, consider giving a half-day off on Fridays.

- Consider a compressed weekly schedule such as a 4-day work week instead of the traditional 5-day.

- Support and endorse working from home one day per week.

- If a parent is involved in the community, consider providing one or two paid days off for them to participate.

- Hold "Bring your family to work" days annually or quarterly.

- Ensure there is an accommodating "on-and-off ramp" policy for employees who may leave the company to spend time with family. Seek to make their re-entry into work easy if they show an interest in coming back.

Re-Entering the Workforce

Women returning to work face a unique set of challenges. Whether they have taken a break from work due to illness, for family or for education, women looking to re-enter the workforce may experience a loss of confidence, fear, shame and trepidation. [92] If a working woman has taken a break to raise her family, there is generally no set end date for this type of sabbatical. It could be anywhere between a few months to years.

From a poll of 3,000 working parents, LinkedIn and Censuswide found that almost half of new mothers take extended maternity leave. Further to that, the survey also found that 75% of those women wanted to take an extended leave but didn't due to financial restrictions. Women who do end up taking a career break do so for about an average of two years. However, eventually, almost 40% of those women returned to the workforce with 4 in 10 of those women having their return dictated by their finances. [93]

Mother's Pay Gap, the Maternal Wall and Imposter Syndrome

So, when these women actually take the steps to return to the workforce, they may firstly experience the

---

[92] Tracy Saunders, "The Return to Work Syndrome: The Unique Challenges Women Face Reentering the Workforce," TLNT, December 19, 2018, https://www.tlnt.com/the-return-to-work-syndrome-the-unique-challenges-women-face-reentering-the-workforce/

[93] Caroline Fairchild, "Nearly Half of Mothers Work, Take a Break, and Work Again. Why Is There Still Such a Stigma?," LinkedIn, March 4, 2020, https://www.linkedin.com/pulse/nearly-half-mothers-work-take-break-again-why-still-stigma-fairchild/

"mother's pay gap" or the "maternal wall." [94] When looking for work as a mother, you may encounter difficulties in negotiating salary or finding work with sufficient pay. Deborah J. Swiss and Judith P. Walker introduced the "maternal wall" in 1993 as the mother's equivalent to the glass ceiling, explaining "— that is, the inability to advance in their careers based on stereotypes of mothers' abilities and commitment to work."[95] And this is further proven by the pay gap between mothers and fathers. The US census found in 2017 that women's yearly earnings fall after the birth of a child and do not recover until the child reaches the ages of 9 or 10. Meanwhile for men, their yearly earnings do not experience this same initial decrease and instead increase steadily over time as the child ages. [96]

Another major challenge that women re-entering the workforce experience is a detrimental blow to their confidence called, "imposter syndrome." Dr. Pauline R. Clance introduced this phenomenon in 1978 and defined it as ambitious and successful individuals plagued with the fear of being uncovered as a "fraud,"

[94] Saunders, "The Return to Work Syndrome: The Unique Challenges Women Face Reentering the Workforce."

[95] Deborah J. Swiss and Judith P. Walker, Women and the Work/Family Dilemma: How Today's Professional Women Are Confronting the Maternal Wall (New York: Wiley, 1994).

[96] YoonKyung Chung et al., The Parental Gender Earnings Gap in the United States, Center for Economic Studies: Washington, 2017, https://www2.census.gov/ces/wp/2017/CES-WP-17-68.pdf

due to the inability to take credit for their successes and achievements. [97] This ultimately leads to confidence loss. This is likely one of the biggest challenges that women returning to work experience - the drop in confidence. To begin with, women are more uncomfortable and less confident when it comes to telling potential employers about their accomplishments in their previous workplaces or in group projects. [98] This especially becomes difficult when women have been on career breaks, and they may view it as a time where their contributions cannot be quantifiably translated into valuable workplace skills. This again comes back to confidence. Though your skills in child rearing or those that you garnered through education or volunteering were not obtained within the workplace, it does not mean that they cannot be *applied* to the workplace.

Women looking to re-enter the workforce should look to their soft skills and a way to quantify their accomplishments whether it be organizing a school fundraiser, leading a group project, or volunteering at a community event. Try not to sell yourself short. However, you still may find yourself apprehensive

---

[97] Saunders, "The Return to Work Syndrome: The Unique Challenges Women Face Reentering the Workforce."

[98] Michelle C. Haynes and Madeline E. Heilman, "It Had to Be You (Not Me)!: Women's Attributional Rationalization of Their Contribution to Successful Joint Work Outcomes," *Personality and Social Psychology Bulletin 39*, no. 7 (2013): 956-959, https://journals.sagepub.com/doi/abs/10.1177/014616721348 6358?journalCode=pspc

during your job search. This combination of a transition to a new lifestyle, a lack of confidence and owning your accomplishments plus a system that limits earning potential for mothers can be detrimental to women looking to return to work.

There are two other challenges that may really affect women returning to work. The first is called the "skill deterioration theory" which was presented by Katherine Weisshaar in 2018 as the idea that when employees were absent for a period of time from work and not utilizing their skills this led to these employees losing their skills from lack of use therefore making them less valuable than other potential hires.[99] Not only is this a theory from Weisshaar's study but women also report feeling that they will not have the skills necessary to return to a modern workforce. [100]

The second challenge prior to even getting into the office, also presented by Weisshaar, is "signaling theories." This speculates that when employers are looking through candidates' profiles, they look for certain details and "signals" such as employment gaps which they then use to make assumptions about potential employees. Weisshaar found that a period of

---

[99] Katherine Weisshaar, "From Opt Out to Blocked Out: The Challenges for Labor Market Re-entry after Family-Related Employment Lapses," American Sociological Review 83, no. 1 (2018): 34-60, https://journals.sagepub.com/eprint/wss5qdJRASWnqYiQiBpp/full

[100] Fairchild, "Nearly Half of Mothers Work, Take a Break, and Work Again. Why Is There Still Such a Stigma?."

unemployment resulted in fewer job opportunities for those looking to return to work. Further, Weisshaar stated, "Put simply, stay-at-home parents were about half as likely to get a callback as unemployed parents and only one-third as likely as employed parents."[101]

It is difficult enough to be a job seeker as someone who has just been on a career break; however, if you are able to re-enter the workforce after a period of absence you may be met with another set of challenges. This may include feeling initially lost in the new environment, adjusting to a lower salary than you may expect, feeling out of touch with your co-workers, and renegotiating childcare and housework. [102]

With each of these new challenges comes several new actionable strategies that women in leadership and those re-entering the workforce can use to accomplish

[101] Katherine Weisshaar, "Stay-at-Home Moms Are Half as Likely to Get a Job Interview as Moms Who Got Laid Off," Harvard Business Review, February 22, 2018, https://hbr.org/2018/02/stay-at-home-moms-are-half-as-likely-to-get-a-job-interview-as-moms-who-got-laid-off

[102] Sue Shellenbarger, "When Getting the Job Is the Easy Part," The Wall Street Journal (Dow Jones & Company, February 17, 2010), https://www.wsj.com/articles/SB10001424052748703798904575069590202587252

their goals and overcome their hardships. Consider the following strategies from *Women Who Money*:[103]

- **Prepare** - This will be a transition that will be met with many challenges, so it is important to try and be ready ahead of time. This could involve updating or creating an entirely new resume, writing cover letters, and contacting references before you begin applying for jobs. It is crucial that you do not try to hide or be dishonest about career breaks on your resume. You may want to check some online resources or local employment agencies if you are feeling particularly lost around resume and cover letter writing. Some online resources include: The Muse, Monster, or Women for Hire. You may also consider checking in with your local library or your college career services office - you may have access to certain alumni services.

- **Learn** - If you're looking at your resume and you feel that it has some gaps, you may want to look at the field that you wish to re-enter and the most desirable skills for those who are successful. A career advisor may also recommend further training or education prior to re-entering the workforce. This could involve checking with community centers, community colleges or development centers for low-cost courses to garner new skills or fine-tune old ones. But your

---

[103] Vicki Cook and Amy Blacklock, "What Is The Best Advice For Returning To The Workforce?," Women who Money, October 19, 2020, https://womenwhomoney.com/best-advice-returning-work/

professional development may also include obtaining certifications or licenses (online or in person), attending conferences or volunteering. Perform as much research as you are able about the jobs you are interested in. This will help dispel any doubts that an employer may have about the gaps in your resume.

- **Connect -** This may be a difficult step for some who have had longer career breaks and been out of the workforce for a lengthy period as this is the time to begin reaching out to former colleagues and other people in your field. Even if you haven't had recent contact, most people are quite receptive to being taken out for coffee or lunch to discuss careers and where you are in life. Look to them for advice on how you can prepare to return to the workforce that you left. Some things you may want to ask about include: company culture, management styles, technology integration and day to day tasks.

  However, if you are re-entering the workforce and your hope is to gain a position in a different field than you left, you may want to consider finding someone who works in that field through friends or family or online. You may want to send them a lunch invitation and be upfront that you'd like to speak to them about their work. *Women Who Money* advises to "be sure to ask what they both enjoy and dislike about their work." These steps of taking someone out for lunch or coffee may put you out of your comfort zone; you could also consider attending a workshop or an online webinar to make connections in new or familiar fields of work. But it is imperative that you begin building your network as a woman re-entering work. According to a LinkedIn Survey performed in 2016, over 85% of all jobs filled between 2015 and 2016 were through networking. [104]

- **Socialize** - After making some in-person connections, you may want to turn to social media to begin connecting and socializing with others in your field or soon-to-be field. If you don't have a LinkedIn profile, now could be the time to make one that highlights your skills and experience because, nowadays, 87% of recruiters use LinkedIn to review candidates.[105]You can use Facebook or Twitter to let your friends and followers know that you are looking for work. This is an essential step. Almost 8 out of 10 job seekers, according to Glassdoor, advised that they are likely to use social media in their career search. [106] You can also start to demonstrate your skills and what makes you hirable on your social media feed as job leads could come from anywhere and you never know when a

---

[104] Lou Adler, "New Survey Reveals 85% of All Jobs Are Filled Via Networking," LinkedIn, February 29, 2016, https://www.linkedin.com/pulse/new-survey-reveals-85-all-jobs-filled-via-networking-lou-adler/

[105] *Jobvite Recruiter Nation Report 2016: The Annual Social Recruiting Survey*, (Jobvite: Indiana, 2016), https://www.jobvite.com/wp-content/uploads/2016/09/RecruiterNation2016.pdf

[106] Chris Skaggs, "Going Inbound for Talent Acquisition - Glassdoor for Employers," US | Glassdoor for Employers, July 18, 2020, https://www.glassdoor.com/employers/blog/going-inbound-talent-acquisition/

recruiter may be perusing your profile. Twitter is a great platform for making connections and searching businesses. Once you've made an account, follow potential employers as well as local career centers and the university or college that you attended.

Also, look out for online workshops or webinars to attend that may be posted and shared by online employment agencies. Even if social media is not the key factor in your re-entering of the workforce, it can prove beneficial to familiarize yourself with the platforms. It is virtually impossible to find companies in this day and age that are not at least present on social media and in 2017, it was determined that 90% of businesses in the U.S. were marketing through social media. [107] Therefore, building your online presence may be a crucial step in your re-entry to the workforce.

- **Adapt** - You may need to be flexible and compromise when looking for a new position to launch back into your career. You may be looking at careers or fields that involve factors that you never considered such as contracting or term instead of traditional full-time work. Carol Fishman Cohen, cofounder and CEO of iRelaunch, a company that focuses on helping women wishing to return to

---

[107]Astrid Guttmann, "U.S. Social Media Marketing Reach 2019," Statista, May 13, 2019, https://www.statista.com/statistics/203513/usage-trands-of-social-media-platforms-in-marketing/

work after a career break, says to consider "three C's." She states,

> The key things to evaluate before starting the process are control (your schedule), content (what your job will be) and compensation (will I be paid what I am worth?). You may have to compromise on one if you've been out for a long time, such as trading some compensation in order to have more control or flexibility. But you should never have to compromise on more than one.[108]

So be flexible and adapt based on what is available in the current job market but try to only compromise on one of the C's outlined by Fishman Cohen. If your situation allows for it, be open to a variety of options as you may find that your needs have changed over the time of your career break.

- **Interview** - It may be quite nerve-wracking to walk into your first interview after a career break. Preparation and being proactive are critical steps in feeling ready and less anxious. With the current state of social media and the internet, it is easier than ever to find specific

---

[108]Shelley Zalis, "What You Need to Know About Taking A Career Break," Forbes (Forbes Magazine, January 30, 2018), https://www.forbes.com/sites/shelleyzalis/2018/01/30/the-truth-about-career-breaks/?sh=55eaf77e2a7d

companies, their mission, clients and competitors. This is a crucial step. Learn as much as you can about the company you are interviewing with as one of the first questions you may hear in your interview is: "what do you know about our company?" It may also be worthwhile to check the website Glassdoor which includes reviews from previous employees and potential information about salary for employees in similar positions.

Fortunately, the other recommended steps in preparing for an interview have likely not changed much since before your career break. You should create a list of potential questions and outline your responses to those questions. Ask a family member, friend, or previous colleague to assist you with a mock interview. You can also try recording your answers to analyze your tone, body language and clarity. Prepare several examples of how you have succeeded in your previous career as well any volunteer or part-time work that you have completed since then. Try to choose examples that best represent a combination of your skills, making note of any areas that you feel you need to improve in case the employer asks. It is very likely that an employer will ask you about your career break, so it is absolutely imperative that you prepare for this.

How to Explain your Career Break in an Interview

Do not hide from it. Your career break should be clearly outlined on your resume. Attempt to show that you are open to talking about it when it is brought up through body language (relaxed and smiling) and tone (vibrant and enthusiastic). After you've set a positive approach with your body language and tone, ensure that you structure your answer beforehand. You can use the following formula outlined by Shamanth Pereira in the Talented Ladies Club blog:

- Start with why you chose to take a break
- Discuss what you did during your break with examples
- Summarize how your career break experiences will benefit you in this role.[109]

Pereira goes one step further and shares her example answer when she was asked about her career break:

My reason for taking time out is to build a strong foundation for my young family. I wanted to make the most of their formative years and be there in the early stages of their development.

During this time, I completed an MBA and built an e-commerce business from scratch. I always wanted to continue my intellectual curiosity

[109]Shamanth Pereira, "A Simple Formula for Explaining Your Career Gap in a Job Interview," Talented Ladies Club, May 29, 2017, https://www.talentedladiesclub.com/articles/a-simple-formula-for-explaining-your-career-gap-in-a-job-interview/

whilst taking on my role as a mother, though I wanted the flexibility to manage it on my own terms.

So, freelancing and building my own business allowed me to achieve both. It was certainly much trickier creating boundaries and certainly taught me the fine art of being productive in a short time space and the ability to work amongst chaos.

So, throw me in any situation and I will thrive, and I certainly look forward to bringing onboard these skills and experience to this role.[110]

After addressing the interviewer's questions about your skills, career break and experience, complete the interview successfully by asking a few questions of your own. Always seek to prepare at least one or two questions for the employer to show that you are interested in the position, that you have prepared fully and that you are ready to return to the workforce.

- **Demonstrate -** All of the steps above will help you prepare for the application process and simultaneously, they should help to build your confidence when re-entering the workforce. As discussed previously, women are notoriously less confident as outlined by Katty Kay and Claire

---

[110] Pereira, "A Simple Formula for Explaining Your Career Gap in a Job Interview."

Shipman in the Atlantic and "the confidence gap." [111] The network connections that you established beforehand will also assist with your ability to speak confidently and to finally demonstrate your skills when you re-enter the workforce. You will be bringing in skills not only from your previous work experience but also from your career break. Do your best to not underestimate your value that you are bringing to the company. You have already shown perseverance and an ability to adapt by re-entering the workforce after an extended break. Quite possibly, there will be aspects of your new job that will be unfamiliar but being confident in the skills that you do have can assist with identifying any weaknesses and asking for clarification when you need it. *Women who Money* states that, "lacking confidence is one of the major stumbling blocks for people returning to the workforce. You don't want to come across as arrogant, nor as timid."[112] Therefore, you may need to strike a balance between demonstrating your confidence and skills while still showing you are eager to learn, adapt and grow in this new career.

- **Humble** - This point and the previous one should be addressed concurrently. Though you should be confident, it is important to remain humble as if you

---

[111] Katty Kay and Claire Shipman, "The Confidence Gap," The Atlantic (Atlantic Media Company, August 26, 2015), https://www.theatlantic.com/magazine/archive/2014/05/the-confidence-gap/359815/

[112] Cook and Blacklock, "What Is the Best Advice For Returning To The Workforce?"

are returning after a long break it is possible that your new colleagues and managers may be younger and even less experienced than you. From 2011 to 2017, the millennial workforce has increased to 38 % making them the largest workforce generation in the United States. [113] It may be an adjustment from what you previously knew of workforces and corporate structure. You should focus on your skills and what you bring to your position that will in turn benefit the company as a whole. Ask questions when you are dealing with an unfamiliar problem and consider that you may need to adapt to a new way of working. Your prior experience and background as a woman in leadership will come through as you rebuild your career even though you may have had to accept a lower salary or position than you expected. One of the most important aspects for finding harmony between demonstrating confidence and humility is asking for feedback about your job performance. According to a study by Gallup in which they surveyed over 65 000 employees, they found that turnover rates were 14.9% lower in companies where employees received strengths feedback versus those that received none. [114] Therefore, seek

[113] Terry Sheridan, "Millennials Now Make Up Largest Workforce Generation in US," AccountingWEB, November 17, 2017, https://www.accountingweb.com/practice/growth/millennials-now-make-up-largest-workforce-generation-in-us

[114] Jim Asplund and Nikki Blacksmith, "The Secret of Higher Performance," Gallup.com (Gallup, May 3, 2011), https://news.gallup.com/businessjournal/147383/secret-higher-performance.aspx

to meet with your manager on at least a weekly basis to check in on your performance and what you can do to improve as an employee in order to make the transition back into the workforce as smooth and as productive as possible.

Chapter 4: ADVOCATE: How to Succeed as a Leader Who Champions Diversity

Overview

As you navigate through different stages of life, you may need to implement different strategies as your position changes, and you grow as an individual. However, it is not only different stages of life that may hold you back from accomplishing your goals. There is still a clear disparity between the sexes especially for women in management but there are other inherent societal barriers that you may encounter as an immigrant woman leader, as a woman leader of color, as a member of the LGBTQIA2S+ and/or as a woman leader who suffers from anxiety or mental illness. These challenges should be addressed one by one and it should also be considered that personal experiences will greatly vary.

Immigrant Women Leaders

No matter the immigration story, many women in leadership who are immigrants experience several barriers when moving to a new country to restart their lives. Not only may they be met with citizens unwilling to accept them, but they will face further difficulties when entering the workforce. Many of those who are immigrating to the United States are well-educated, professional workers and this is increasing. According to the Pew Research Center in 2016, 17.2% of immigrants over 25 had a bachelor's degree and an additional 12.8% had a postgraduate degree. Since 1980, the percentage of immigrants with their bachelor's degree has more than doubled while those with their postgraduate degree have increased by over 40%. Comparatively with the U.S. born population, the rates of those with their undergraduate is almost exactly the same. [115]

In 2015, Naila Meraj of the University of Western Ontario performed a study on the "settlement Experiences of Professional Immigrant Women in Canada, USA, UK and Australia." [116] The study provided an in depth look at the experiences of highly skilled immigrant women and the challenges that they experienced while settling into these four countries. Meraj discovered several recurring themes throughout this study that included:

- discrimination
- deskilling
- professional immigrant women as trailing spouses

[115]Jens Manuel Krogstad and Jynnah Radford, "Education Levels of U.S. Immigrants Are on the Rise," Pew Research Center (Pew Research Center, September 14, 2018), https://www.pewresearch.org/fact-tank/2018/09/14/education-levels-of-u-s-immigrants-are-on-the-rise/

[116] Naila Meraj, "Settlement Experiences of Professional Immigrant Women in Canada, USA, UK and Australia," Electronic Thesis and Dissertation Repository, (University of Western Ontario, 2015). https://ir.lib.uwo.ca/etd/2700

- lack of social support
- difficulties related to cultural and environmental adjustment
- impact of immigration on physical and psychological health
- positive and ambivalent experiences of immigration and settlement.[117]

Workplace discrimination was discovered to be the most prevalent issue that professional immigrant women experience. This included reports of hostile and unprofessional behavior, sexual harassment, racist bullying and discrimination due to language barriers. In addition to this discrimination on the job, immigrant women also reported feeling discriminated against prior to even entering the workforce. In Canada, the demand for local Canadian work experience was viewed as a form of discrimination as it was keeping these professional immigrant women out of the workforce. Further, in Australia, those women seeking employment found that employers seemed to not trust their overseas qualifications. [118] This discrimination goes further. Nurses in both the UK and Australia advised that they experienced discrimination based on their lack of English skills. Not only did it make communication challenging but it implicated their relationships at work in a negative way. These professional women felt that they were labelled as "foreign" due to their accents and finite knowledge of

---

[117] Meraj, "Settlement Experiences of Professional Immigrant Women in Canada, USA, UK and Australia."

[118] Meraj, "Settlement Experiences of Professional Immigrant Women in Canada, USA, UK and Australia."

the local culture. This has caused many professional immigrant women to feel socially isolated both at work and in their community. Grace Vaccarelli, a lawyer at the Human Rights Legal Support Centre in Ontario says,

> "You can't discriminate based on someone's accent. If the person can do the job, then accent is an irrelevant factor." She continues, "There's no grey area... [Accent] really is a proxy. People say accent, but what they're really saying is someone from the Global South. You don't hear the Queen's English being used in the same way [when] you hear other accents."[119]

Interestingly enough, though immigrant women are explicitly discriminated against due to a variety of factors, Meraj found that there is an "implicit recognition" of immigrant women's "competence" by their co-workers and managers. [120] These immigrant women were directed to take on more authority and responsibilities when other employees were absent.

---

[119] Lakshine Sathiyanathan and Lisa Xing, "An Accent Might Keep You from Getting Hired Even Though It's Not Supposed to, Advocate Says | CBC News," CBCnews (CBC/Radio Canada, January 23, 2018), https://www.cbc.ca/news/canada/toronto/the-accent-effect-toronto-3-1.4409181

[120] Meraj, "Settlement Experiences of Professional Immigrant Women in Canada, USA, UK and Australia."

They did not receive any additional compensation for their work but they were trusted for their competence even though these skills would not be acknowledged by their colleagues or by managers in the form of compensation. [121]

Many immigrant women who are highly-skilled experience deskilling when they arrive in a new country. Immigrant women are highly-educated.[122] Just over a quarter of Canadian-born women have their bachelor's degree. Comparatively, half of immigrant women who have arrived in Canada in the last five years have their bachelor's degree or higher. 60% of those women in that pool are working in positions that do not require a degree in comparison to 30% of Canadian-born women with the same qualifications.[123] They may be forced to take a job different or lower than expected due to their qualifications and skills not being recognized by domestic employers. This is due to a variety of structural and societal barriers. It has been suggested by Hiebert in 2005 that this deskilling is due to a detachment between immigration policy implemented by the state or province and the credential process regulation and control by professional associations. Overall, it is a disconnection

---

[121] Meraj, "Settlement Experiences of Professional Immigrant Women in Canada, USA, UK and Australia."

[122] Tamara Hudon, "Immigrant Women," Government of Canada, Statistics Canada, March 3, 2016, https://www150.statcan.gc.ca/n1/pub/89-503-x/2015001/article/14217-eng.htm.

[123] Hudon, "Immigrant Women."

between the overarching government bodies and the associations that actually regulate entry to desirable professions. [124] Therefore, despite the need for professionals in the economy like medical professionals, there are still gaps that women immigrants could fill but they are buried by red tape and downward social and economic mobility. Dr. Komal Ambaliya, a professional immigrant woman working towards becoming a doctor in Canada, says,

"I just give [the] advice ... that if you are [in] the medical profession, don't come. And if you come, don't expect to work in the field of what you have worked before. It's almost impossible, despite [the] shortage of doctors."

It's discouraging and disheartening for those who have studied for years in their home country to only be met with barrier after barrier. If immigrant women do attempt to receive accreditation for their overseas qualifications, it is often an awfully expensive and lengthy process. Due to this separation between government and professional associations, the policies for accreditation have not been amended therefore many professional immigrants are only able to enter their field if they complete post-migration education. This education can vary. It may include an examination

---

[124] Daniel Hiebert, "Winning, Losing and Still Playing the Game: The Political Economy of Immigration in Canada," Tijdschrift voor Economische en Sociale Geografie 97, no. 1 (2006):38–48, 10.1111/j.1467-9663.2006.00494.x

or it may involve repeating full courses or degrees. Many professional immigrant women are forced to take this route in order to reconcile their careers in a new workforce. [125]

Immigrant women that manage to break through the barriers above and garner a position in executive leadership make up a small percentage. In the Greater Toronto Area which employs thousands of people across a multitude of sectors, only 6% of executives are immigrants. [126] The Toronto Region Immigrant Employment Council (TRIEC) released a report in 2018 citing not only the lack of immigrants in executive positions but that for immigrant women it was even worse. Even though overall, women made up 36% of the executives in the region, racialized immigrant women made up only one in 100 corporate executives. The report referred to this barrier for newcomers as the "sticky floor."

Though most countries like Canada, USA, U.K. and Australia will offer support to immigrants and newcomers when they first arrive, there is little support to advance their careers and to gain executive-level positions. This has in turn led to a salary income

[125] Meraj, "Settlement Experiences of Professional Immigrant Women in Canada, USA, UK and Australia."

[126] *Building a Corporate Ladder for All: The Case for Advancing Immigrant Talent in the Greater Toronto Area,* (Toronto Region Immigrant Employment Council: Tornoto, 2019), https://triec.ca/wp-content/uploads/2019/11/Building-a-Corporate-Ladder-for-All-final.pdf

gap for immigrants that increases with age. The TRIEC report says, "As immigrants age, and hypothetically reach more advanced stages in their careers, their incomes should align more closely with people born here. Yet, the salary income gap seems to be growing with age."[127] In the Greater Toronto Area, immigrants between the ages of 35 to 44 are earning about a quarter less than Canadian-born workers of the same age. This increases to almost 40% less than their Canadian counterparts by the time they reach ages 45 to 54. Furthermore, the report advises that immigrants are severely lacking in senior executive mentorship who can offer guidance with potential promotions. They note that "organizations are not investing in grooming these workers for leadership." [128]

How to Promote a More Equal and Inclusive Workforce

For professional immigrant women who want to break through the "thick glass ceiling" or get off the "sticky floor," [129] organizations must begin to include leadership development programs, professional development strategies and inclusion training for those already in leadership positions. The following

---

[127] TRIEC, "Building a Corporate Ladder for All: The Case for Advancing Immigrant Talent in the Greater Toronto Area."

[128] TRIEC, "Building a Corporate Ladder for All: The Case for Advancing Immigrant Talent in the Greater Toronto Area."

[129] TRIEC, "Building a Corporate Ladder for All: The Case for Advancing Immigrant Talent in the Greater Toronto Area."

are six strategies for how to promote equality in the workforce and lead a more inclusive organization:

1. **Set targets** - Consider setting diversity and inclusion targets for immigrant women. This should involve holding staff accountable for diversity and inclusion initiatives. Human resources may need to shoulder some of these responsibilities but all staff should play a role in building a more inclusive workplace culture. Try to attribute these targets with tangible statistics so that you can monitor the progress of staff, evaluate when necessary and frequently communicate when changes need to be made. [130]

2. **Educate Leaders** - Prior to implementing professional development for all staff, leaders should be trained first. According to the TRIEC in almost all successful cases of implementation of diversity and inclusion policies it involves change that stems from the top and from leadership teams that are committed to inclusion goals. Regardless of the leader's gender, ethnicity or immigration status, these executives should work to unleash the potential of their employees by empowering an inclusive workplace culture.

---

[130]Yilmaz Dinc, "How Far Have Immigrant Women Advanced in the Workplace?," Canadian HR Reporter (Canadian HR Reporter, March 8, 2019), https://www.hrreporter.com/opinion/hr-guest-blog/how-far-have-immigrant-women-advanced-in-the-workplace/298685

This begins with knowledge and acknowledgment but companies should work towards strategically nurturing diversity in the workplace. Firstly, the leaders require the knowledge of inclusivity and they should be capable of acting upon it in order to actively implement this with their staff. Leaders should have an understanding of what stage their organization is in and then design interventions based around the companies and employee's needs. According to TSNE (Third Sector New England), the seven phases of diversity in the workplace are as follows:

- o Phase 1: Prepare for Start-Up
- o Phase 2: Establish a Framework
- o Phase 3: Early Implementation
- o Phase 4: Integration
- o Phase 5: Evaluation
- o Phase 6: Redefinition
- o Phase 7: Consolidation[131]

Which phase is your organization currently in? Are your leaders aware and equipped with the tools needed in their respective phase? Some organizations may want to consider further leadership training programs such as TRIEC's Certificate in Inclusive Leadership and Inclusive

---

[131] "Diversity and Inclusion Initiative: A Step By Step Guide." TSNE MissionWorks, 2010.
https://www.tsne.org/diversity-and-inclusion-initiative-step-step-guide

Workplace Competencies or the Diversity & Inclusion Certificate Program from the American Management Association.

3. **Offer Professional Development** - Once leaders are adequately trained and knowledgeable about how to better support diversity, all other employees can participate in professional development programs to help create a more inclusive workplace culture. The type of program you choose may depend on the needs of your organization but many of these learning opportunities can enable you as a woman in leadership to take a strategic approach to creating a diverse and inclusive environment. This training should also involve tracking who has accessed these professional development opportunities so when times for promotion come immigrants, women and people of color will all have a fair chance at advancement. Tracking also allows for identifying trends of possible biases that exist in the organization and it can lead to a gender gap analysis that recognizes areas of strength, weakness and opportunity. It also can call attention to gaps in compensation among marginalized groups, and reflect on the hiring and advancement process which could include some gender or race-based biases. It is important to include an assessment of the hiring process as though leaders may look to make changes immediately and promote women immigrants from within; organizations should strive for long-term, sustainable change.

4. **Adopt Flexibility** - Immigrant women experience many barriers. Discrimination, language, accreditation issues and access to childcare. A child care desert is an area in which there is inadequate licensed child care available in that region. Half of Americans live in child care deserts. Immigrant families, Hispanic and Native American, Alaskan Natives and rural families disproportionately make up the populations that live in child care deserts, forcing fewer mothers to participate in the labor force and presenting further barriers to newcomers. [132] So, it is crucial that employers present a flexible arrangement for women and immigrant women in order to help overcome this challenge. This may include providing return to work initiatives after a woman takes a career break, telecommuting, and/or flexible working hours.

5. **Use an Intersectional Lens** - The TRIEC report states that "Organizations need holistic talent management and [diversity and inclusion] strategies that include immigrants as part of their efforts to diversify their talent pipelines and move towards more inclusive workplaces." [133] Therefore, it is not just the implementation

---

[132] Rasheed Mailk et al., "America's Child Care Deserts in 2018," Center for American Progress, December 6, 2018, https://www.americanprogress.org/issues/early-childhood/reports/2018/12/06/461643/americas-child-care-deserts-2018/

[133] TRIEC, "Building a Corporate Ladder for All: The Case for Advancing Immigrant Talent in the Greater Toronto Area."

of the practices we discussed above in order to leverage immigrant talent but it also involves looking at practices and initiatives implemented in the past with an intersectional lens. One interviewee from the TRIEC report advised that even though organizations had put in place gender inclusion initiatives that they often ended up centering around white women. [134] Therefore, excluding racialized women and racialized immigrant women. The barriers put up in front of immigrant women are complex, variable and incredibly taxing; therefore, organizations should implement solutions that are equally intricate and interconnected between all levels of the organization. This involves a holistic approach accepted by all staff that includes accountability on how immigrant women and other marginalized groups are treated by executives, middle-management and all staff.

Many of these strategies rely on organizational and societal change in order to improve prospects for immigrant women. However, it is important to look at real cases of immigrant women in leadership to see how they have overcome all the barriers that faced them.

Before arriving in the United States, Chinwe Esimai spent 17 years in Nigeria. Today she is a Harvard-educated lawyer who spearheads global initiatives to

---

[134] TRIEC, "Building a Corporate Ladder for All: The Case for Advancing Immigrant Talent in the Greater Toronto Area."

fight corruption. She is a regular speaker at the United Nations and at several respected seminars, workshops and other international organizations. Today she is the Managing Director at Citi as the Chief Anti-Bribery and Corruption Officer. She has spent much of her extraordinarily successful career inspiring other immigrant women to overcome their barriers and propel themselves forward in their careers. Chinwe refers to these women leaders as "American Dream Queens."[135] She is personally familiar with all of the barriers faced by immigrant women and by those who are juggling childcare, motherhood and work. Chinwe says:

> "You may not be everything and
> everywhere at the same time. Being
> an executive is a full-time job, being a
> mom is also a full-time job, and being
> a wife is part-time at the minimum.
> It's a lot of jobs and the expectations
> don't go away. It's about how you
> think about it and how you manage
> it". [136]

---

[135]Africh Royale, "Meet Chinwe Esimai: the Harvard-Trained Lawyer Passionate about Inspiring Generations of Immigrant Women Leaders," Africhroyale, October 25, 2019, https://africhroyale.com/meet-chinwe-esimai-the-harvard-trained-lawyer-passionate-about-inspiring-generations-of-immigrant-women-leaders/

[136] Royale, "Meet Chinwe Esimai: the Harvard-Trained Lawyer Passionate about Inspiring Generations of Immigrant Women Leaders."

Chinwe has outlined certain traits that she has noticed in herself and in other expat powerhouses that have helped her to excel in American organizations. Firstly, that immigrant women have an instinct to blend in and downplay their differences, but that they must ignore it. Instead, Chinwe advises that immigrant women must stand out and demonstrate their strengths and formidable characteristics to forge their path to success. She says: "I would not be able to lead the initiatives I have against bribery and corruption if it weren't for my experiences making me the person I am...It'd be impossible."[137]

Secondly, Chinwe says that successful immigrant women make an effort to eradicate self-limiting behaviors and excuses. Immigrant women can often be labelled as "outsiders" in their workplace and in the communities.[138] Unfortunately, these labels from the community and by others can also affect the way you perceive yourself. If you begin to identify with these labels, it can lead to self-limiting outcomes. For example, you may feel uncomfortable speaking up when promotions arise or feel that you do not have the qualifications or language skills to succeed. We can attach these labels to ourselves and use them as

---

[137] Merilee Kern, "Expat Leadership: Lessons All Professionals Can Learn from Hugely Successful Immigrant Women," Thrive Global, July 10, 2019, https://thriveglobal.com/stories/expat-leadership-lessons-all-professionals-can-learn-from-hugely-successful-immigrant-women/

[138] Kern, "Expat Leadership: Lessons All Professionals Can Learn from Hugely Successful Immigrant Women."

justifications for our choices. Esimai suggests "rigorous self-examination" to overcome these labels and self-limiting behaviors. She states, "all the great leaders I know...they're constantly thinking about where they want to be, what they want to achieve and how to get there."[139]

The third trait that Esimai outlined was the ability of other successful expats to define themselves. Many people that you meet throughout your career will make judgements about you and your work ethic. They may try to label you and place you in categories based on your background, education, and experience. Esimai notes that extraneous and potentially damaging advice is "inevitable."[140] So immigrant women should avoid trying to blend in avoid limiting themselves based on societal labels and do their best to define themselves as current and future women in leadership.

Try looking for role models like Esimai who carved her own path through and around the multitude of challenges presented to immigrant women. When speaking about these challenges and trying to find herself in a country she wasn't born in, Esimai provides some sound advice,

> I think one of the most important
> things I will say is don't let any of

[139] Kern, "Expat Leadership: Lessons All Professionals Can Learn from Hugely Successful Immigrant Women."

[140] Kern, "Expat Leadership: Lessons All Professionals Can Learn from Hugely Successful Immigrant Women."

your differences stop you from bringing your full self. Understand your unique talents, understand your gifts, and step into what it is you want to do, and don't let anything that makes you different as an immigrant stop you from doing that. Because I know a lot of people sometimes hold back because they say "Well, when I get rid of my accent, I'll do this", or "When I am fully integrated, I can then pursue my dreams". I think it's important to engage right away because everyone's voice is important.[141]

Women of Color in Leadership

Immigrant women and women of color face many similar challenges when it comes to garnering promotions and lack thereof in diversity and inclusion policies. However, their experiences cannot be equated as there are complex challenges facing both groups that are affected by multifaceted personal and economic factors. Women of color represent 18% of the U.S. population[142] and they are expected to make up the

---

[141] Royale, "Meet Chinwe Esimai: the Harvard-Trained Lawyer Passionate about Inspiring Generations of Immigrant Women Leaders."

[142] Zuhairah Washington and Laura Morgan Roberts, "Women of Color Get Less Support at Work. Here's How Managers Can Change That.," Harvard Business Review, March 4, 2019, https://hbr.org/2019/03/women-of-color-get-less-support-at-work-heres-how-managers-can-change-that

majority of all women by 2060. [143] This means that they could also become the majority of the future U.S. workforce. Women of color entrepreneurs generate $361 billion in revenue, launching companies 4 times faster when compared to other women-owned businesses. [144] Yet despite the ambition and drive of women of color's leadership, only 4% of c-level positions are made up of women of color according to a 2018 report. White women, on the other hand, are more than 4 times as likely to be in a c-level position. [145] Even those who are highly educated still face the glass ceiling that many women find when trying to garner an executive level position. Between 1977 and 2015, 532 black women received their MBAs from Harvard Business School yet only 13% of them achieved a top-level executive position. Comparatively, 19% of black men and 40% of non-black Harvard

---

[143] Cindy Pace, "How Women of Color Get to Senior Management," Harvard Business Review, August 31, 2018, https://hbr.org/2018/08/how-women-of-color-get-to-senior-management

[144] The 2017 State of Women-Owned Business Report, (American Express, New York, 2017), https://ventureneer.com/wp-content/uploads/2017/11/2017-AMEX-SWOB-FINAL.pdf

[145] "Women Business Leaders: Global Statistics," Catalyst, August 11, 2020, https://www.catalyst.org/research/women-in-management/

Business School alumni obtained this highest-ranking executive role. [146]

Women of color are highly ambitious and goal oriented as many women in leadership are. A Nielsen survey found that 64% of Black women's goal was to make it to the highest level in their profession which was nearly double that of non-Hispanic white women. It was also reported that compared to 75% of men and 68% of white women, 83% of Asian women, 80% of black women and 76% of Latinas were yearning for a promotion. [147]

Sayu Bhojwani, the Founder and President of New American Leaders, details three more challenges for women of color in leadership that have led to exhaustion in the fight for change to political organizations, private companies, media rooms and nonprofits. Firstly, Bhojwani advises that the "scarcity mindset" has led to women of color feeling pressured to hold tight to leadership opportunities as these opportunities are few and far between. She advocates that women of color and immigrant women are already familiar with doing more for less but that this has also translated into professional life where they are being underpaid for the "greater good" and taking less time

---

[146] Laura Morgan Roberts et al., "Beating the Odds," *Harvard Business Review March-April*, (2018): 126-131, https://hbr.org/2018/03/beating-the-odds

[147] Sarah Coury et al., "Women in the Workplace 2020," McKinsey & Company (McKinsey & Company, September 30, 2020), https://www.mckinsey.com/featured-insights/diversity-and-inclusion/women-in-the-workplace

off for fear that there is not enough time to do so. She says, "We feel guilty caring for ourselves, or even for a child or loved one. We associate success with how dependable and available we are. And before we know it, success and burnout become one and the same. This scarcity is rooted in fear, and that fear breeds competition." [148]

Secondly, Bhojwani cites another major challenge for women of color as the competition for "crumbs." For example, if you were to visit an office that works in technology and computer-science, women make up only 25% of those related roles. Within that quarter, only 5% are Asian women, 3% are Black women and 1% are Hispanic. [149] This has led to a possible perception from office workers and by women of color that diversity has become an "only one in the room" phenomenon. "We internalize the idea that there is room at the table for just one of us, in part because we have explicitly been shown as much," Bhojwani notes. "In the non-profit world specifically, funders contribute to our stress by doling out grants in small amounts, suggesting that there are too many organizations meeting the same mandates." This can lead to a feeling of competition amongst women

---

[148] Sayu Bhojwani, "Why Women of Color Leaders Are So Tired," TwentyThirty, March 4, 2020, https://twentythirty.com/article/women-of-color-leaders-sayu-bhojwani/

[149] Nikki Graf, Richard Fry, and Cary Funk, "7 Facts about the STEM Workforce," Pew Research Center (Pew Research Center, January 9, 2018), https://www.pewresearch.org/fact-tank/2018/01/09/7-facts-about-the-stem-workforce/

leaders of color for not only higher-level positions but for support and for recognition. [150] Despite the importance of role models and support networks for women in leadership, women of color are being pitted against one another in an internal competition set forth by organizations and funders. As Bhojwani points out this competition can in turn lead to further exhaustion and feelings of inadequacy. This leads to her third point regarding challenges that women of color are experiencing, the feeling of being inadequate. Bhojwani advises that women of color can "obsess" over what could have been done differently in order to reach their accomplishments leading to persistent feelings of not being good enough. And even when they are able to reach and accomplish some of their goals such as reaching a top 100 list, Bhojwani says "we are complicit in creating a celebrity culture that keeps some people at the top rung of the ladder and some at the bottom." So, it is important that women of color try to dispel these thoughts of inadequacy and advocate for themselves as there may be barriers that persist due to societal expectations and stereotypes.

The importance of advocating for oneself becomes even more important for women of color as according to a McKinsey and Leanin study; they receive less support from managers. [151] Their bosses are less likely

---

[150] Sayu Bhojwani, "Why Women of Color Leaders Are So Tired," TwentyThirty, March 4, 2020, https://twentythirty.com/article/women-of-color-leaders-sayu-bhojwani/

[151] "Women Business Leaders: Global Statistics," Catalyst, August 11, 2020, https://www.catalyst.org/research/women-in-management/.

to promote the contributions that they make to the team, to assist them with organizational politics and to spend time with them outside of office hours. When being left out of this informal network, this can lead to a loss or an inability to build a meaningful support network. Role models and sponsorship are critical for moving up the corporate ladder for diverse leaders. [152]However, Bhojwani notes that women of color should take heed as if they do manage to get recognition for their accomplishments and overcome feelings of inadequacy with or without a support network, it comes at a cost. She says,

> I have found myself code-switching, performing Whiteness, at first unknowingly, and then on purpose, for the sake of my organization and leadership. These acts are often passive — not innocent, but passive. Like smiling politely during cocktail conversations filled with microaggressions or wearing our clothes and hair a certain way in order to blend in. And, when pressured to keep up, many of us have made active choices to do things that are contradictory to our communities and our values. We

---

[152] Audrey J. Murrell and Stacy Blake-Beard, Mentoring Diverse Leaders: Creating Change for People, Processes, and Paradigms (New York, NY: Routledge, 2017).

> sacrifice our sense of selves and may
> even lose sight of our core values.

[153]It is somewhat of a balancing act for women of color in leadership. Bhojwani has detailed several barriers that could affect many women in leadership, so it is important to look for some actionable strategies to work towards a better, more inclusive and less exhaustive workplace.

Aleia Walker, a former web developer and now Digital Marketing Specialist, offers some advice for being the "only one" in the room:

- **Get someone on your side** - As discussed, it can be incredibly difficult for a woman of color to build up a support network even from their own managers. Walker suggests that having a mentor or an experienced ally is "almost necessary" when entering teams where they may be outnumbered and want to be prosperous. Find a mentor who is experienced working and navigating in the same environment that you are working in. Consider that this mentor may be different from you especially for women of color in male-dominated industries. You may find that your options may be limited to white males or women but consider that this may be to your benefit. This could allow you to view your environment through a different lens and

---

[153] Sayu Bhojwani, "Why Women of Color Leaders Are So Tired," TwentyThirty, March 4, 2020, https://twentythirty.com/article/women-of-color-leaders-sayu-bhojwani/

consider diverse perspectives when approaching a problem. Women of color have advised that even with a cis white male as their mentor that they have learned to, "approach solutions in ways that allowed them to be more assertive." [154]

- **Begin with Inclusivity** - Walker advises that before even applying for jobs in your industry that you should look at the posting to see if the position is actually inclusive and prioritizes diversity. If you are already working actively in your position as a leader, you may want to review your organization's diversity & inclusion policies. Joblint is a tool that scans job postings for you to ensure that the descriptions are not riddled with sexism or cultural and recruitment issues. You may want to try job boards like Professional Diversity Network or Diversity.com to find postings that prioritize and value diversity.

- **"Ask the Right Questions"** - Whether you are already working in leadership or if you are looking for a position in leadership as a woman of color you should take the steps to ask questions from your organization to determine what they value. You should consider asking about diversity & inclusion programs as well as possible professional development available to you. A question Walker advises that all Black women and their allies ask is: "What do you continue to do as a company to

---

[154] Aleia Walker, "We Need to Talk About Being the 'Only One' in the Room," Skillcrush, accessed November 2, 2020, https://skillcrush.com/blog/only-one-in-the-room/

educate your staff on anti-racism and support organizations dedicated to ending police brutality against Black people?"[155] A company's response to this question may give a comprehensive view of an organization's perspective on the repression and injustice against Black women and men. It will also provide insight into how a company may treat or treats vulnerable persons and it can help indicate how you may expect to be treated as a woman of color.

As a current woman in leadership, you may want to consider asking this same question to your employees and management. Consider how racial injustice has been approached internally and externally and what companies can do going forward in order to support marginalized employees.

If you are not a woman of color and instead are a woman in leadership wondering how you can support, consider some of the actions and strategies below.

- **Extend Help** - The phenomenon of being the "only one" in the room can be very taxing on women of color. With the barriers discussed above, women of color may decide not to participate in out of work activities like happy hour and other social events. They also may avoid sharing personal details when compared with white women and men. [156] As a

---

[155] Walker, "We Need to Talk About Being the 'Only One' in the Room."

[156] Katherine W Philips, Tracy L Dumas and Nancy P Rothbard, "Diversity and Authenticity," *Harvard Business Review*

woman in leadership, a personal invitation could go a long way. Advise your employee that you would like to get to know them better and encourage them to participate in social gatherings. Appropriate personal outreach is an important step in the building of women of color's support network and reaching their workplace goals in the future.

- **Give Credit** - In 2010, a study by Amanda Sesko and Monica Biernat found that Black women were more likely to be "unnoticed" and "unheard." When compared to Black Men and White women and men, Black women sharing in a group discussion were less likely to be correctly attributed and credited.[157] This has led to a common feeling of invisibility at work for women of color. It is crucial that women in leadership recognize this bias and make note of it if it occurs in their workplace especially when a woman of color's work is possibly going unnoticed or underappreciated. You may also want to consider highlighting her contributions through several different channels so that the woman of color has a record that she can later use to assist her with advancement.

- **Provide Honest Feedback** - Some managers have struggled to give women of color effective and

---

March-April, (2018): 132-136,
https://hbr.org/2018/03/diversity-and-authenticity

[157] Amanda K Sesko and Monica Biernat, "Prototypes of Race and Gender: The Invisibility of Black Women," *Journal of Experimental Social Psychology 46*, no. 2, (2010): 356-360, https://doi.org/10.1016/j.jesp.2009.10.016

honest feedback for fear of being perceived as racist. [158] This only presents further barriers for women of color in the future. Though it can be difficult to share constructive and honest feedback, it is an essential managerial skill that shows that managers care about their employee's personal growth. [159] You should take the steps to note areas of improvement but ensure the employee knows that you are paying attention to both their strengths and weaknesses. Dan Coyle recommends the following prompt for feedback in his book The Culture code, "I'm giving you this feedback because your part of this group and we care about you and we think that you can do better at...."[160]

- **Consider Potential** - When looking to promote and advance some for your employees, few may have all the competencies you desire for a role in leadership. It is important to consider widening your candidate pool not just based on competencies but based on the potential of the candidates. Egon Zehnder has created a model that looks at a

---

[158] Shelley J Correll and Caroline Simard, "Research: Vague Feedback Is Holding Women Back," Harvard Business Review, April 29, 2016, https://hbr.org/2016/04/research-vague-feedback-is-holding-women-back

[159] "Radical Candor - The Surprising Secret to Being a Good Boss," First Round Review, accessed November 26, 2020, https://firstround.com/review/radical-candor-the-surprising-secret-to-being-a-good-boss/

[160] Daniel Coyle, Culture Code: The Secrets of Highly Successful Groups (New York, NY: Random House Business, 2019).

candidate's potential to grow both personally and professionally; it assesses the future competence of those that may move into leadership roles. Zehnder's model assesses the following four traits for determining a candidate's potential: curiosity, insight, engagement and determination.

Looking to the present, the readiness of a candidate, their fit between the requirements of the role and the current state of their traits includes their competencies, identity, culture fit and personality. Therefore, competency is only one factor of four that could be considered when assessing a candidate's career trajectory. And finally, when determining a candidate's future, the four traits (curiosity, insight, engagement and determination) that help you predict this can tell you not only the possible executive ability of the candidate but also the speed at which they may develop.[161] Therefore, when looking to advance employees, look not only to their competencies as this may exclude women of color and other marginalized groups, and instead consider assessing their potential.

- **"Check for Bias"** - Only 18% of companies check for bias in reviews based on both race and gender. Though organizations are making strides to check possible gender bias at a rate of 42% in reviews and promotions, companies should begin actively checking and tracking potential biases in the

---

[161] Gerhardt and Riedel, "When Assessing Talent, the Essential Thing Is to Look at an Executive's Potential to Grow, Both Professionally and Personally."

promotion and hiring processes for women of color. [162] This may involve keeping data sets that include the velocity at rate at which women of color are hired and promoted versus their colleagues in your organization. For example, consider measuring the responsibilities of a manager who was recently promoted and compare that to an Asian woman who was recently advanced. Are there responsibilities the same? Who has driven more or less business growth? What was the size of their respective teams? Without tracked data, cases in which there is a large disparity may go unnoticed. You may also want to consider the implicit bias within your corporation that affects the hiring and promotion processes. An implicit bias is a stereotype or attitude that individuals have towards certain groups of people that they are not consciously aware of. The impacts of implicit bias can be detrimental to women of color. A recent study that explored how racial minorities were treated in the Canadian workforce found that between two Asian groups with equivalent qualifications and experience those with names that implied their ethnicity were selected almost a third less than those with English-style names. [163]

---

[162] Women in the Workplace 2020, (McKinsey & Company, New York, 2020), https://wiw-report.s3.amazonaws.com/Women_in_the_Workplace_2020.pdf

[163] Rupa Banerjee, Jeffrey G Reitz and Phil Oreopoulos, "Do Large Employers Treat Racial Minorities More Fairly? A New Analysis of Canadian Field Experiment Data," *Canadian Public Policy* 44, no.1 (2018): 1-12, https://doi.org/10.3138/cpp.2017-033

Women in leadership should examine their own implicit bias. Considering and recognizing these potential internalized prejudices can lead to an overall less biased hiring and promotion process.

- **Perform Exit Interviews** - When technical specialist Qichen Zhang left Google after racist comments from a co-worker she said, "I didn't see a lot of women, especially Asian women, black women or other women of color in the executive ranks. I didn't see any opportunities for myself ... The culture there is really discouraging, and that's ultimately why I left." Very few companies have implemented mandatory exit interviews to find out why their employees have moved on even though they could be a source of incredibly useful anecdotal data especially when it comes to diversity and inclusion policy implementation.

These interviews can provide candid insights into the experiences of women of color and how to improve the experience for all employees. If your human resources team seems hesitant to take on this task, an exit interview is something you can informally perform as a woman in leadership. You may find information on possible conflicts within your organization and employees, and you may also discover discriminatory behaviour that you weren't aware of. Dr. John Sullivan, an expert in retention, advises that exit interviews are one of his first recommendations to employers due to the fact that they are "intuitive, low cost, easy to implement,

130

and they produce spectacular results."[164] This could in turn lead to a more diverse, inclusive and productive experience for future women of color and all employees as a whole.

Members of LGBTQIA2S+ in Leadership

LGTBQIA2S+ is an acronym for Lesbian, Gay, Bisexual, Transgender, Queer and/or Questioning, Intersex, Asexual, Two-Spirit and affirmative ways in which people choose to self-identify.

On June 15, 2020, that the Supreme Court of the United States ruled that the protection of employees from discrimination on the basis of sexual orientation or gender identity should be protected under the Civil Rights Act of 1964. [165] Prior to this ruling, 28 of the 50 states in America had no state-level protection for gender identity and sexual orientation, meaning almost half of LGBTQIA2S+ workers in the states were without statutory protections. [166] Despite this, many

---

[164]John Sullivan, "Improve Retention Up to 50 Percent Because Post-Exit Interviews Get More Honest Answers," Dr. John Sullivan, August 8, 2017, https://drjohnsullivan.com/articles/improve-retention-50-percent-post-exit-interviews-get-honest-answers/

[165] Adam Liptak, "Civil Rights Law Protects Gay and Transgender Workers, Supreme Court Rules," *The New York Times* (The New York Times, June 15, 2020), https://www.nytimes.com/2020/06/15/us/gay-transgender-workers-supreme-court.html

[166] Kerith J. Conron and Shoshana K. Goldberg, "LGBT People in the US Not Protected by State Non-discrimination Statutes," (The Williams Institute, California, April 2020).

countries still do not provide LGBTQIA2S+ workers with any legal protections, only 77 countries have prohibited employment discrimination based on sexual orientation. [167] Even now that these protections have been put in place by the Supreme Court, LGBTQIA2S+ Americans are still experiencing discrimination in their workplace and when applying for jobs. In fact, during the job application process one-fifth of LGBTQIA2S+ Americans have experienced discrimination based on their gender identity and/or their sexual orientation with 32% of LGBTQ people of color experiencing this same discrimination at a higher rate. And if there is any LGBT+ indicators on a woman's resume, a recent study from New York University found that they would be 30% less likely to get a phone call from employers. A researched on the study, Emma Mishel explains, "When you look at my work history, it's a lot of LGBT organizations, so it's pretty obvious that I'm queer." [168]

When on the job, 22% of LGBTQIA2S+ Americans have not been promoted at the same rate of their colleagues nor paid equally. It is not only a matter of experiencing

---

[167] Lucas Ramón Mendos, State-Sponsored Homophobia 2019: Global Legislation Overview Update, (ILGA World, December 2019): 101-113:
https://ilga.org/downloads/ILGA_World_State_Sponsored_Homophobia_report_global_legislation_overview_update_December_2019.pdf

[168] Tim Gibson, "How Gay Women Are Treated in the Modern Workplace," myGwork, accessed November 26, 2020, https://www.mygwork.com/en/my-g-news/how-gay-women-are-treated-in-the-modern-workplace

these discriminatory barriers prior to entering the workforce but these stereotypes and biases continue in the workplace as well. The U.S. Equal Employment Opportunity Commission considers any offensive jokes based on sexual orientation and/or gender identity as a form of harassment. [169] Despite this these microaggressions are common for LGBTQIA2S+ workers, more than half have heard lesbian and gay jokes, 37% have heard bisexual jokes and 41% have heard transgender jokes. Transgender employees have reported that that have been harassed and bullied at workplaces in China. Over 21% of transgender workers have reported experiencing discrimination in China. It is important to note that LGB workers experience different types of harassment than transgender workers. Transgender workers could experience limitations on their bathroom accessibility, being deliberately labelled with their incorrect pronouns, and feeling pressured to answer and tolerate inappropriate and personal questions. [170]

It has been found that LGBT workers are prevented by fear of this discrimination to be their full authentic

---

[169] "What You Should Know: The EEOC and Protections for LGBT Workers," | U.S. Equal Employment Opportunity Commission, accessed November 26, 2020, https://www.eeoc.gov/laws/guidance/what-you-should-know-eeoc-and-protections-lgbt-workers.

[170] Joel Rudin et al., "Bigenderism at work? Organizational Responses to Trans Men and Trans Women Employees," *Organizational Management Journal 17*, no. 2 (2020): 63-81, https://www.emerald.com/insight/content/doi/10.1108/OMJ-02-2018-0507/full/html

selves at work. In the United States, almost half of LGBTQIA2S+ workers are closeted with 59% of non-LGBTQIA2S+ employees believing that sexual orientation or gender identity discussion in the workplace are "unprofessional." [171] Therefore, a perpetual challenge that LGBTQIA2S+ workers are experiencing is downplaying or hiding their personal relationships, possibly hiding the way they dress or speak in order to avoid being seen as unprofessional and in order to avoid discrimination. [172]

In the UK, a study was completed by the British LGBT Awards including 1200 lesbian and bisexual women from across the country. They found that 64% of these women had experienced sexual discrimination, inappropriate language, and lack of opportunities or bullying at their workplaces. Further, 73% advised that they were not entirely out to colleagues. They also advocated for the need of more lesbian and bisexual women in leadership roles in order to provide more opportunities for mentorship and to boost visibility with more than 86% of women supporting this notion.

---

[171] Deena Fidas and Liz Cooper, A Workplace Divided: Understanding the Climate for LGBTQ Workers Nationwide (Human Rights Campaign, 2019): p. 6, https://assets2.hrc.org/files/assets/resources/AWorkplaceDivided-2018.pdf

[172] Sejal Singh and Laura E Dorso, "Widespread Discrimination Continues to Shape LGBT People's Lives in Both Subtle and Significant Ways," Center for American Progress, May 2, 2017, https://www.americanprogress.org/issues/lgbtq-rights/news/2017/05/02/429529/widespread-discrimination-continues-shape-lgbt-peoples-lives-subtle-significant-ways/

The founder of the British LGBT Awards, Sarah Garret, says:

> The results are startling and clearly
> show that in 2016 lesbian and gay
> women are still finding it hard to be
> themselves in the workplace and
> worse still, those who are out at
> work have had negative experiences
> including discrimination, bullying
> and reduced opportunities to
> progress compared to male
> counterparts. The findings are
> worrying and show that a lot of work
> remains to be done to change
> attitudes and promote acceptance.[173]

Another barrier that may seem to actually be in gay women's favor but still seems rooted in societal prejudices and stereotypes is the "gay pay gap. In 2010, an Industrial Relations study found that gay women earn on average 6% more than straight women. However, gay women still earn less than gay men who, in turn, still earn less than straight men. [174] Despite this pay gap being in the favor of gay women over straight women, lesbian couples are still more likely to live

---

[173] Gibson, "How Gay Women Are Treated in the Modern Workplace."

[174] Nicole Denier and Sean Waite, "Sexual Orientation Wage Gaps across Local Labour Market Contexts: Evidence from Canada," *Industrial Relations 72*, no. 4 (2017): 734 10.7202/1043174ar

under the poverty line than heterosexual couples. [175] Joe Pinsker of the Atlantic theorized that this gap in pay may exist because of a "larger trend that favors masculinity in the workplace. Gay men are still out-earning straight women, and lesbians, who may be, "Perceived as less feminine and closer to the unencumbered male ideal."[176] This theory and the pay gap in itself rely on specific stereotypes and discrimination that surrounds LGBTQIA2S+ employees.

Even though gay women on average earn more than straight women, there is still a thick glass ceiling that LGBTQIA2S+ women experience when seeking executive level positions. According to Mckinsey's Women in the Workplace research, LGBTQIA2S+ women are less represented than women in general in corporate America. Only four of America's largest companies' CEOs are LGBTQIA2S+ of which only one is a woman. [177] Though it is difficult to estimate the

[175] M.V. Lee Badgett, Laura E Durso and Alyssa Schneebaum, "New Patterns of Poverty in the Lesbian, Gay and Bisexual Community," (The Williams Institute, California, June 2013).
https://williamsinstitute.law.ucla.edu/wp-content/uploads/Poverty-LGB-Jun-2013.pdf

[176] Katty Kay and Claire Shipman, "The Confidence Gap," The Atlantic (Atlantic Media Company, August 26, 2015), https://www.theatlantic.com/magazine/archive/2014/05/the-confidence-gap/359815/

[177]Diana Ellsworth, Ana Mendy, and Gavin Sullivan, "How the LGBTQ Community Fares in the Workplace," McKinsey & Company (McKinsey & Company, June 23, 2020), https://www.mckinsey.com/featured-insights/diversity-and-

percentage of LGBTQIA2S+ citizens in the United States, approximately 5.1% of U.S. women identify as a part of the LGBTQIA2S+ community while 3.9% of U.S. men identify as LGBTQ+. [178] However, the representation in corporate America is significantly different especially within top-level management. Only 0.6% of senior vice-presidents and c-suite level executives are LGBTQIA2S+ women compared to 2.9% of LGBTQIA2S+ men.

LGBTQIA2S+ women experience a steady decrease in representation from entry level through to management and executive level. This decrease begins with the first promotion to management level as while they comprise 2.3% of entry level employees, they only make up 1.6% of managers.[179] This can lead to further lack of role models and mentorship for LGBTQIA2S+ employees and to feelings of isolation in the workplace. Further to this, the "only one in the room" may affect LGBTQIA2S+ employees similarly to how it affects women of color and immigrant women. With small numbers in representation, they are likely to represent

---

inclusion/how-the-lgbtq-plus-community-fares-in-the-workplace.

[178] Female LGBT proportion of population: United States LGBT Data & Demographics, (Williams Institute, California, January 2019), https://williamsinstitute.law.ucla.edu/visualization/lgbt-stats/

[179] M.V. Lee Badgett et al., "Bias in the Workplace," Williams Institute, June 2007, https://williamsinstitute.law.ucla.edu/publications/bias-in-the-workplace/

their entire group when attending meetings or events at work.

As discussed previously and as represented by research, this "only one in the room" phenomenon can induce an increase in stress and it can cause more microaggressions from other employees when you are the only one representing your group specifically for women. [180] Additionally, LGBTQIA2S+ women are twice as likely as other women to report being the "only one in the room," and compared to straight white men they are seven times more likely to say so. While LGBTQIA2S+ women of color are eight times more likely to report being the only representative of their demographic. [181]

Therefore, LGBTQIA2S+ women are susceptible to a variety of challenges especially when trying to reach their executive aspirations. They are 1.5 times more likely than straight men to cite that the opportunity to be a mentor or role model for other LGBTQIA2S+ women plays an important part in their motivation to advance their own careers. They are also 1.4 times more likely to seek executive leadership roles in order

---

[180] Kevin Sneader and Lareina Yee, "One Is the Loneliest Number," McKinsey & Company (McKinsey & Company, January 29, 2019), https://www.mckinsey.com/featured-insights/gender-equality/one-is-the-loneliest-number

[181] Ellsworth, Mendy, and Sullivan, "How the LGBTQ Community Fares in the Workplace."

to make a positive impact on the world compared to straight men. [182]

Challenges for Transgender Individuals

When discussing the challenges of the LGBTQIA2S+ community in the workplace, it is important to recognize the differences and distinct challenges faced by those who identify as transgender or for those who identify with a gender other than the one assigned at birth.

It is estimated that 1.4 million people in the United States identify as transgender, and they have an unemployment rate at three times higher than the U.S. average.[183] They face several distinct challenges including a lack of social protections, high levels of harassment and discrimination and the constant feeling of "only one in the room." This feeling of being the only one is much more likely to be reported by those who are transgender. They are also over 10% less likely to have the support of a mentor or a sponsor to help them through these feelings of isolation. [184]

---

[182] Ellsworth, Mendy, and Sullivan, "How the LGBTQ Community Fares in the Workplace."

[183] Lily Zheng and Alison Ash Fogarty, "Why You Still Have No (out) Trans People at Your Company," Quartz at Work (Quartz, June 18, 2018), https://qz.com/work/1308079/how-to-be-inclusive-of-trans-people-in-the-workplace/

[184] Ellsworth, Mendy, and Sullivan, "How the LGBTQ Community Fares in the Workplace."

Transgender people also face the glass ceiling when looking towards advancement, similar but distinct from those who identify as lesbian, gay, bisexual or queer. In the largest American companies, there are no individuals who identify as Transgender at the senior vice-president or c-suite level positions. [185] They are less likely to have responsibilities that relate to management, evaluation and hiring, and they are more likely to view their gender or sexual orientation as a barrier to their advancement. [186]

Effective Strategies for Supporting LGBTQIA2S+Workers

As women in leadership break through barriers to higher-level positions, it may be time to look back at their organizations for meaningful progress towards supporting LGBTQIA2S+ workers. According to Great Place to Work and Pride at Work Canada, 85% of organizations have a team or a person in place whose mandate explicitly includes the support of LGBTQIA2S+ employees and 81% of those organizations have access to funding to implement these supports. [187] These following strategies below

---

[185] Badgett et al., "Bias in the Workplace."

[186] Ellsworth, Mendy, and Sullivan, "How the LGBTQ Community Fares in the Workplace."

[187] Alison Grenier and Jacq Hixson-Vulpe, *Beyond Diversity: An LGBT Best Practice Guide for Employers,* (Great Place to Work and Pride at Work Canada, Toronto, 2017), https://prideatwork.ca/wp-content/uploads/2017/09/Beyond-Diversity-LGBT-Guide.pdf

can help women in management lead their teams and organization towards a more supportive environment for LGBTQIA2S+ workers:

- **Write it Down** - Firstly, it is essential to check that your organization's policy formally addresses and outlines anti-discrimination and harassment as it relates to sexual orientation, gender identity, and gender expression. These policies should provide examples of what possible homophobic, bi-phobic and transphobic language and actions may look like. Further, seek to make these policies widely available and accessible through your staff files and communications. This could also include the individuals who are responsible for compliance and their role in the implementation and enforcement of these policies. If you live in Canada, communicating these policies to your employees is required by human rights legislation. In the United States, back in 2002, only 3% of Fortune 500 companies had discrimination policies in place that protected gender identity and sexual orientation. In 2020, 91% of companies have these policies in place. [188] Another important step that should not be missed when evaluating your company's policies is their review process. Policies should be up to date to ensure the language is current, that it is up to date based on government legislation, and reflective of the values of your organization.

---

[188] *Corporate Equality Index 2020: Rating Workplaces on Lesbian, Gay, Bisexual, Transgender and Queer Equality,* (Human Rights Campaign Foundation, Washington, 2020), https://www.hrc.org/resources/corporate-equality-index

According to Great Place to Work and Pride at Work, you may want to review your discrimination policies every 3 to 5 years. [189]

- **Address Inappropriate Behaviors** - There are a few steps that organizations and women in leadership can take in order to prevent discrimination and microaggressions against LGBTQIA2S+ employees. The first may be to include company-wide diversity and inclusion behaviors so that employees can recognize inappropriate behaviors within others and themselves. This may include a review of the companies' policies, respectful versus harmful language including use of pronouns and names, and how your organization's safe-reporting channels will lead a discrimination and/or harassment investigation that is witnessed or experienced by employees. These safe-reporting channels should be created to investigate and immediately address inappropriate behaviors. You can take the steps to advise all employees of these channels so that they feel comfortable in addressing these potentially harmful behaviors and microaggressions. Above all, as a woman in leadership, you should try to advocate having measures in place for all levels of the organization (especially management and executive level) with appropriate behaviors modeled for each level to help integrate this training into the day-to-day functions of your workplace.

---

[189] Grenier and Hixson-Vulpe, *Beyond Diversity: An LGBT Best Practice Guide for Employer.*

- **Minimize the 'only' experience** - As discussed, many marginalized groups are susceptible to the isolating feelings of being the "only one in the room." Women in leadership and management can help to minimize these experiences by proactively highlighting the organization's support of LGBTQIA2S+ community and initiatives. This can not only provide some reassurance to current LGBTQIA2S+ employees but also to prospective future employees. The "only" experience can also be reduced through human resources processes and broadening the pool of candidates as well ensures that this diversity and inclusion is being tracked so that this data can later be evaluated. A strategy to consider is blind resume-screening. This means that those who are recruiting will remove names, signifiers of gender and group affiliations to reduce the potential of affecting the process with implicit bias. Katherine McNamee, the director of Human Resources at the American Alliance of Museums (AAM) implemented a blind resume process into her organization and instead assigned applicants a number and refers to them as such until they are brought in for an interview.

> "It has changed our mindset as an organization," McNamee says. "We're more aware of hiring biases. We've clarified our evaluation criteria. And because we've taken a collaborative approach to blind hiring, I think it has improved the candidate's

143

experience with our hiring process."
[190]

Another strategy that could be used to reduce the feelings of onlyness can be to strengthen or implement resource groups for LGBTQIA2S+ employees. In order to develop an Employee Resource Group (ERG) you may want to look for an executive champion or sponsor one from within your own organization. If you are part of the LGBTQIA2S+ community or if you consider yourself an ally, you could consider becoming this executive champion yourself. Preferably, the executive champion that is chosen should have a personal connection to LGBTQIA2S+ issues and challenges. It was found by the Corporate Equality Index in 2018 that 97% of LGBTQIA2S+ ERGs are sponsored by an executive champion who acts as a liaison between the resource group and the executive-level management of the organization. 60% of these champions identified as allies while 38% of them identified as openly LGBTQ+.[191]

- **Implement Structural Support for Transgender Employees** - Organizations should begin to

[190] Daniel Bortz, "Can Blind Hiring Improve Workplace Diversity?," SHRM (SHRM, March 20, 2018), https://www.shrm.org/hr-today/news/hr-magazine/0418/pages/can-blind-hiring-improve-workplace-diversity.aspx

[191] "Establishing an Employee Resource Group," HRC, accessed November 26, 2020, https://www.hrc.org/resources/establishing-an-employee-resource-group

address and make steps towards improving the distinct challenges that transgender employees face. A 2011 survey from Transgender PULSE stated that for employees who transitioned at work only 20% of their colleagues were always accepting of their new gender identity. It was reported that 15% never received acceptance from their co-workers, and 13% of the participants reported getting fired because they were transgender. [192] Women in leadership can advocate for making health care inclusive in order to prevent health barriers from arising that may affect a trans employee's career. Being a trans employee supporter may also involve supporting leave for those who are transitioning and allowing the use of washrooms in which the employee feels the most comfortable, integrating a gender-neutral washroom if possible. Women in management may also want to ensure that human resources systems allow changes to employee documents and records and that the documents are inclusive of all genders and pronouns. You can also contemplate setting up transgender employees with sponsors if available in order to support advancement in their careers and providing training to other employees around transgender issues.

---

[192]Greta Bauer et al., "We've Got Work to Do: Workplace Discrimination and Employment Challenges for Trans People in Ontario," *Trans PULSE E-Bulletin 2*, no. 1 (2011), https://transpulseproject.ca/wp-content/uploads/2011/05/E3English.pdf

- **Provide Options & Flexibility** - Working from home poses unique challenges for a variety of groups but for those who are already experiencing feelings of isolation due to their gender identity or sexual orientation, they may find these issues magnified in a remote work environment. Video conferencing such as within Zoom meetings can reveal certain parts of employee's homes or lives that they may not be comfortable with. Women in management may want to have conversations with all of their employees beforehand to determine their boundaries between their personal and professional life. Online meetings can also further feelings of isolation as it is easy for the loudest voices to dominate discussions. This challenge can be combated if leaders establish a support network and clear communication with any and all employees that may be experiencing marginalization or isolation.

There also may be a need to perform a re-evaluation on the norms of a virtual work environment that fosters inclusivity. This could include, rotating speaking roles in virtual meetings and providing scheduled downtime so that LGBTQIA2S+employees and all employees can take the time to focus on their personal needs. Therefore, a remote work environment can be an incredibly positive experience for LGBTQIA2S+ workers if they are supported by their employers despite the fact that it may perpetuate some feelings of isolation when initially moving into a virtual environment. Further, it was shown by Flexjobs and Remote-how that almost all of the best companies for LGBTQIA2S+ workers offer the opportunity for flexible work. [193] It is an additional strategy to ease LGBTQIA2S+ worker's stress and it provides an option for transgender employees who may be in the midst of transitioning. Sarah Brown, a transgender activist and specialist on LGBTQIA2S+ issues, advises,

> ...remote working can be helpful for enabling greater flexibility for LGBT communities; this could be both for getting into work and for staying engaged in the workplace. Remote working may be particularly useful when LGBT people are transitioning or dealing with mental health issues, but also in a more general sense as it creates a safe space to carry out a job without having to worry about the other factors which intersect within the typical workplace.[194]

Women Leaders & Mental Health

Women are nearly twice as likely to be diagnosed with an anxiety disorder than men. [195] The reasons for this have been speculated by a variety of studies. It could be because of a difference in hormone fluctuations and the

---

[193] Marek Grygier, "Struggling to Include More LGBT+ People? Remote Work Will Help!: Remote-How," Remote, June 2019, https://remote-how.com/blog/struggling-to-include-lgbt-remote-work-will-help

[194] Grygier, "Struggling to Include More LGBT+ People? Remote Work Will Help!: Remote-How."

[195] "Women and Anxiety," Anxiety and Depression Association of America, ADAA, accessed November 26, 2020, https://adaa.org/find-help-for/women/anxiety

chemistry in our brains. It could be linked to hormonal changes during events like pregnancy which have been linked to high-levels of anxiety. [196]Pregnancy has even been linked to a higher risk of the development of obsessive-compulsive disorder due to the surge in hormones like oestrogen and progesterone. Further to these biological explanations, women are also more likely to report feeling stressed which increases anxiety. When faced with certain stressful points in life, men and women utilize different strategies to cope. [197] Moreover, women in leadership and executive positions are even more prone to stress, anxiety and psychological distress than men. [198] Sarah Wilson, author and an entrepreneur herself, advises that it is not surprising that anxiety is common among those who are entrepreneurial and in positions where decisions must be made. "It comes down to brain function: their ability to think beyond straight data and to hyper-connect," Wilson says. "They are able to think

---

[196] Emily J. Russel, Jonathan M. Fawcett, and Dwight Mazmanian, "Risk of Obsessive-Compulsive Disorder in Pregnant and Postpartum Women: A Meta-Analysis," *The Journal of Clinical Psychiatry 74*, no. 4 (2012): 377-385, *https://doi.org/10.4088/JCP.12r07917*

[197] Olivia Remes, "Women Are Far More Anxious than Men – Here's the Science," The Conversation, June 10, 2016, https://theconversation.com/women-are-far-more-anxious-than-men-heres-the-science-60458

[198] Millicent H. Abel, "Humor, Stress and Coping Strategies," Humor 15, no. 4 (2002): 365-381, http://web.csulb.edu/~jmiles/psy100/abel.pdf

very broadly across multiple ideas all at once, which lends itself, obviously, to creating a business."[199]

It has also been found by the University of Texas that women in leadership are at a higher risk of depression when compared to men. The research by the Journal of Health and Social Behavior found that when women gained the ability at work to hire, fire, and influence wages they experienced an increase in depressive symptoms such as feelings of sadness or hopelessness, disturbances in sleep and outbursts of anger and frustration. [200] The lead author of the study, Tetyana Pudrovska says, "These women have more education, higher incomes, more prestigious occupations, and higher levels of job satisfaction and autonomy than women without job authority. Yet, they have worse mental health than lower-status women." [201] Pudrovska advises that likely negative stereotypes and gender bias are the source of this disparity. When women move into leadership positions and they become more assertive, the double-bind dilemma arises again. A woman in management can be less assertive, nurturing and be liked by her employees. Alternatively, she can take charge, be assertive, and be

[199] Leigh Buchanan, "All Leaders Have Anxiety. Here's How the Best Ones Deal with It," Inc.com (Inc., May 8, 2018), https://www.inc.com/leigh-buchanan/anxiety-is-the-leaders-best-friend-and-worst-enemy.html.

[200] Stephanie Vozza, "The Discouraging Link Between Depression And Women In Power," Fast Company (Fast Company, January 15, 2015), https://www.fastcompany.com/3040484/the-discouraging-link-between-depression-and-women-in-power.

[201] Vozza, "The Discouraging Link Between Depression and Women In Power."

viewed as competent but she won't be liked. However, she cannot be both. Pudrovska warns that this negative judgment can only further contribute to a woman's chronic stress. [202] Dr. Ruth Sealy at the City University in London agreed with the notion that women in management were "trapped" by traditional views of leadership. She says,

> "Because we assume men's 'natural' competence as leaders, women often have had to work much harder to get to those positions, only to find that even when they get there, their 'right' to that status is continuously questioned." [203]

Effective Strategies for Managing Mental Health Barriers

Despite these mental health barriers, some sources cite anxiety as being a good trait for leaders to have and that it can be used and viewed as strength rather than a weakness. As research continues on this topic, some have found a connection between anxiety and intelligence. A study published in the journal Frontiers in Evolutionary Neuroscience found that those with diagnosed general anxiety disorder exhibited higher IQ

---

[202] Vozza, "The Discouraging Link Between Depression and Women in Power."

[203] Pippa Stephens, "Women Bosses 'More Depressed' than Male Counterparts," BBC News (BBC, November 20, 2014), https://www.bbc.com/news/health-30127275.

scores. Whether the individuals had relatively high or low anxiety, there was a positive correlation found between anxiety and intelligence while it was inverse in those without anxiety. [204] High intelligence could allow leaders with anxiety to be more perceptive and aware of their employees and organizational needs. In fact, in 2013 it was revealed by the Academy of Management journal that those who experience neuroses do better in group settings than extroverts when teamwork is required and experience status-gain due to exceeding expectations in these situations. [205] Through the lens of leadership, anxiety can be an advantage instead of a hindrance. It may become an important part of setting and reaching leadership goals. Scott Stossel draws the conclusion in his book *My Age of Anxiety* that it can lead to the development of effective leadership skills. He advises that "Anxious people, because they are vigilantly scanning the environment for threats, tend to be more attuned than adrenaline junkies to other people's emotions and social signals."

---

[204] Jeremy D. Coplan et al., "The Relationship between Intelligence and Anxiety: An Association with Subcortical White Matter Metabolism," Frontiers in Evolutionary Neuroscience 3, no. 8 (2011), 10.3389/fnevo.2011.00008

[205] Corinne Bendersky and Neha Parikh Shah, "The Downfall of Extraverts and Rise of Neurotics: The Dynamic Process of Status Allocation in Task Groups," Academy of Management Journal 56, no. 2, (2012) https://journals.aom.org/doi/abs/10.5465/amj.2011.0316

How to Transform Anxiety into an Advantage

Women in leadership may want to consider some of the following strategies to assist with fostering their anxiety. Look to the possible advantages of it while simultaneously dealing with the drawbacks of other mental health barriers to become or continue being an effective woman in leadership.

- **Reduce your Choices** - As a leader with anxiety, you may experience situations where making decisions is arduous simply due to the amount of choices. Sarah Wilson says, "If you overtax the decision-making part of your brain, you can trigger anxiety." She notes that those who are anxious may find it almost impossible to make the important decisions if we are weighed down by those that are trivial or less impactful. She suggests keeping 'certainty anchors' throughout your day in order to prevent having to make too many decisions and becoming overwhelmed. This could include things like wearing the same or similar outfits or ordering the same things for lunch so that you don't need to be bogged down by these choices. She also recommends being open with your staff and advising them that if they present a problem to you that they should also present three possible solutions for you to review. Do your best to be clear and keep it to three solutions to prevent a paralyzing amount of choices.

- **Allow yourself Time and Patience** - If you are feeling particularly anxious and that you will not be able to deliver information to your team in a composed manner, you may want to consider developing a support network or mentor that will be able to take on these tasks for you. Consider the way that you best express yourself whether that be through speaking or writing and detail your thoughts to your mentor so that they may be able to relay your message to your employees. If you'd rather deliver the information and communication yourself, you may also want to take some time to refocus and regroup to ensure that you will express yourself in the way that is best for you and your employees.

The link between you and your employees is a very important one and it could be demoralizing to employees to see their leader as fearful or worried. Wilson advises that on days when anxiety is particularly bad even one on one communication can be difficult. This can spiral into feelings of being 'not good enough' despite the fact that you may have reached your goals or are well on your way to do so. Lais Pontes Green notes that she constantly felt that she needed to do more and that she wasn't doing enough as she worked herself up to director level and then eventually started her own business. She gives the following advice to other women who may be feeling this way:

> Feeling 'good enough' should not be how you define success. If you make that your metric, you will always feel less than. Every time you reach one level, you will already have your eye on the next one. And while constant motivation and hard work is an amazing thing, you should take time

to appreciate each level of success.
Celebrate your wins, and take a
breath to congratulate yourself
before jumping on to the next goal.[206]

- **Set Boundaries** - Women in leadership who are anxious may feel a constant pressure to complete work tasks. There may be a constant feeling of urgent responsiveness causing yourself and colleagues to work overtime or on evenings and weekends despite the fact that it may not be entirely necessary. [207] In order to prevent this fear from ruling your workplace, you may need to set boundaries between your work life and personal life. Despite knowing that we should regularly disconnect, many women in leadership feel the pressure to not do so either from societal expectation, from family or from themselves. You should know and decide on your office hours and strictly adhere to that schedule. Responding to emails and texts after work hours can set a tone and pressure on the rest of the organization and employees. Though this may not be your intention, the Center for Executive Excellence advises that "there is nothing more powerful for employees than seeing their leaders model the actions or

---

[206]Lindsay Tigar, "7 Female Leaders on How They Overcame Crippling Anxiety," Ladders (Ladders, March 3, 2020), https://www.theladders.com/career-advice/7-female-leaders-on-how-they-overcame-crippling-anxiety

[207] Joe Baker, "How Good Leaders Manage Anxiety," TLNT, August 11, 2016, https://www.tlnt.com/how-good-leaders-manage-anxiety/

behaviors they are requesting from others."[208] You may want to consider setting up an out-of-office response on your email to really make this message clear.

- **Know yourself and Know Bias** - When you are feeling anxious or if you are under pressure, you may want to consider how your leadership approach is affected. Do you become impatient? Impulsive? Or perhaps you become withdrawn and quiet. Knowing how you react to stress can greatly assist when dealing with employees and complex situations. This may involve asking yourself honest questions and writing down the answers in a journal, paying attention to your inner voice and learning to be forthright with yourself. [209] Also understanding the existence of biases can be an important part of dealing with anxiety as a woman in leadership. Marianne Cooper, sociologist at the Clayman Institute for Gender Research at Stanford University, advises that when women are not aware of the biases that surround them that they can internalize these intolerances as a reflection of their abilities and weaknesses. In actuality, these biases are a reflection of a larger social disparity and dynamic that affects all women in leadership. She says, "They can think, 'Maybe I am too

---

[208] "Leadership by Imitation," executiveexcellence.com, June 6, 2013, https://executiveexcellence.com/leadership-by-imitation/

[209] Kim Aldwin Pana, "Knowing Oneself & Coping with Stress," *KimAldwinPana* (blog), October 10, 2018, https://kimaldwinpana.wordpress.com/

aggressive? 'Maybe I'm not a good communicator?' Once they understand bias, they experience these things differently and take them less personally."

Women in leadership who are experiencing mental health barriers should look to strike a balance between understanding their stressors and understanding societal biases. Lisa Barnett, the president, co-founder, and the chief marketing officer of Little Spoon, gives the following advice to those experiencing anxiety: "Listen, but not too hard. Know the inherent biases with the advice someone gives you and filter accordingly. You should always listen to what other people in your industry have to say, but you don't always have to heed their advice. You know yourself best."[210]

There are a multitude of strategies that women can try in order to cope with mental health strategies; however, there are also several strategies that organizations can implement as well.

For women in leadership who are not experiencing mental health barriers, you can consider the following strategies for providing support to employees who do have these struggles:

- **Eliminate the Stigma** - Organizations and women in leadership can foster open and candid conversations surrounding mental health. This may include acknowledging that these issues readily affect those in management and in leadership roles

---

[210] Tigar, "7 Female Leaders on How They Overcame Crippling Anxiety."

just as they do those in entry-level positions. Bev Gutray, the CEO of the Canadian Mental Health Association in British Columbia advocates for women in leadership to open up about their own mental health. She says, "It opens the conversation for so many people who report to you to get the help that they need." She encourages leaders and supervisors to "create a culture where your managers communicate the message that help is available early, not only for you but for your family."[211] Opening up these conversations could allow for an employee to seek assistance prior to getting to the point of crisis. It may lead to proactive discussions surrounding those employees who are struggling. Women in leadership should seek to normalize these topics in order to prevent these issues spiraling into the stage of crisis. When employees are beginning to show signs such as a decrease in productivity, irritable moods, increased absenteeism and/or short-term and long-term leaves, a safe and stigma-free workplace environment becomes absolutely essential.

- **Acknowledge and Decrease Biases** - After fostering an environment that employees feel safe in to discuss their mental health struggles, women in leadership should consider reviewing their guidelines and policies surrounding mental health in the workplace. You may want to consider asking

---

[211] Carolyn Ali, "Women in Business: Tackling Mental Health in the Workplace," Business in Vancouver, September 20, 2017, https://biv.com/article/2017/09/women-business-tackling-mental-health-workplace

your human resources team to review these policies and those around the hiring process to ensure that they do not include explicit or implicit bias against those who experience mental health barriers. In England, about 40% of people suffering from mental illness advised that they were denied work because of psychiatric treatment history and 60% reported that they have avoided applying for jobs entirely as they expect to be treated unfairly. [212] Further to this, employers were seven times more likely to recommend hiring an employee with a physical disability such as a wheelchair user rather than a person suffering from a mental illness that they require medication for according to one study. [213] The economic repercussions of mental illness are estimated at over $51 billion a year and over 500 000 employees in Canada will not be able to work due to mental illness on any given week.[214] Leaders should strongly consider implementing training for their employees and management on mental health topics to recognize and eliminate these biases that affect employees all over the world.

[212] Kay Wheat et al., "Mental Illness and the Workplace: Conceal or Reveal?" Journal of the Royal Society of Medicine 103, no. 3 (2010): 83-86, 10.1258/jrsm.2009.090317

[213] Wheat et al., "Mental Illness and the Workplace: Conceal or Reveal?"

[214] "Mental Health, Stigma and the Workplace," CAMH, accessed November 5, 2020, https://www.camh.ca/en/camh-news-and-stories/mental-health-stigma-and-the-workplace.

Finally, women leaders can consider the following eight actionable strategies from Workplace Strategies for Mental Health to directly support employees with mental health barriers.

1. **Rule out** the possibility that your employee may be suffering from a mental health concern prior to considering disciplinary action. If you find that they are suffering from mental health barriers, you should support them in a way that will be psychologically safe.

2. **Be aware** of your own implicit bias and do your best to communicate without judgement

3. **Consider your emotional reactions** to an employee's performance or behavior. Do your best to implement emotional intelligence and regulation when dealing with these vulnerable issues.

4. **Focus on outcomes** rather than on the problem. Be especially supportive and clear to avoid any misinterpretation. For example, instead of saying to the employee that their work is "full of errors," you may want to consider solution-focused language such as, "we need this information to be error-free. What do you need to make that happen?" [215]

---

[215]"Supportive Performance Management," Workplace Strategies for Mental Health - Supportive Performance Management, accessed November 5, 2020, https://www.workplacestrategiesformentalhealth.com/managing-workplace-issues/supportive-performance-management

5. **Instead of blaming issues** or problems on personality, try to relate them to the employee's performance and explain the repercussions when that performance is not up to standard. For example, instead of blaming an employee for being disrespectful when they are late to work, you may try, "when you miss the beginning of the work day, you're missing valuable time to discuss and contribute to the issues we'll be dealing with that day. It can also lead to us spending more time to discuss our goals for the day a second time."

6. **Emphasize an employee's strengths** or previous accomplishments first.

7. **Show an understanding** and acknowledgment of the employee's perspective prior to immediately agreeing or disagreeing with their opinion.

8. **Encourage the employee** to develop their own strategies and solutions in order to help them cope with their mental health and build on existing strengths. [216]

Overall, the challenges for women when they belong to these specific demographics, whether it is mental health issues, sexual orientation, citizenship

---

[216] Workplace Strategies for Mental Health, "Supportive Performance Management."

status or race, may have more in common than originally anticipated. These similarities are especially clear when it comes to the actionable strategies for dealing with these challenges in the workplace. There is a substantial amount of evaluations for organizations to consider in their own policies and in regard to their own implicit biases. With the support from their organizations, women in leadership can address their own needs as well as the needs of their employees by fostering a safe, diverse, and inclusive workplace for all marginalized groups.

Chapter 5: EMPOWER: How to Build Your Own Network

Overview

As the gender disparity slowly begins to narrow, women in leadership may be looking for strategies to further diminish this gap by supporting future women leaders. The major step in this being to cultivate other women leaders through the development of skills, networking and through information exchange. There is also much value placed on networking in the workplace that can help to further foster the development of skills and support of women leaders.

Cultivating Women Leaders

With only 6.4% of women making up the CEOs of Fortune 500 companies, there is still a clear gap in c-suite level leadership. However, those that do make it, should look to actively influence and grow the "female executive talent pipeline."[217] If you are in a higher-level of management or c-suite level, you should begin to look to identify ambitious women across your organization's teams. By beginning within your own workplace, you can control and navigate the changes and challenges that these women leaders are facing or

---

[217] Stephanie Harris, "Cultivating Women Leaders Creates a Better Workplace for Us All," Your Dream Blog, August 17, 2018,
https://yourdream.liveyourdream.org/2018/08/cultivating-women-leaders-creates-a-better-workplace-for-us-all/

may face in the future. You may want to look for women on your team with leadership traits like emotional intelligence, excellent communication, and high integrity.

Sheryl Sandberg, the Chief Operating Officer of Facebook and the author of Lean In: Women, Work and the Will to Lead, has given a multitude of talks around the subject of getting more women to the highest level of management. She advises that women should seek to do three things in their careers: "sit at the table, make your partner a real partner and don't leave before you leave." [218]

Sit at the Table

Sandberg discusses attending meetings with other c-suite level managers including women in senior-level management; however, noticing that even those women in high-levels of management did not sit themselves at the table in executive meetings. She attributes this to women notoriously and systematically underestimating their abilities when compared to men. Women are more likely to attribute their success to external factors while men are more likely to credit themselves for their success. Women will look to their colleagues and the people that helped them and while this is seemingly generous and a thoughtful gesture, it is representative of the gap

---

[218] Sheryl Sandberg, "Why We Have Too Few Women Leaders," TED, December 2010, https://www.ted.com/talks/sheryl_sandberg_why_we_have_too_few_women_leaders.

between women and men's confidence in their work. [219] "No one gets to the corner office by sitting on the side of the table," Sandberg says. Perhaps, this fear in confidence stems from the double bind dilemma - in that, if women are able to break through and show confidence and assertiveness then they will be seen as an effective and competent leader, but they will not be liked by their colleagues. There is a cultural expectation for women to be nice, friendly, and to smile, and women going against this societal bias may face the consequences. [220] The unfortunate reality is that success and likeability is positively correlated for men while it is negatively correlated for women. Sandberg experienced this actionable gap in the confidence between genders herself in a Q&A session after one of her talks. An audience member had her hand raised when Sandberg advised that she would take, "two more questions." Upon hearing this the audience member lowered her hand and noticed that the other women in the audience had also lowered their hands, leading to the last two questions being asked by men. Sandberg says,

> And I thought to myself, "Wow, if it's me -- who cares about this, obviously -- giving this talk -- and during this talk, I can't even notice that the men's hands are still raised, and the women's hands are still raised, how good are we as

[219] Sandberg, "Why We Have Too Few Women Leaders."

[220] Caroline Fairchild, "For Women, Being 'Liked' at Work Is a Double-Edged Sword," LinkedIn, July 31, 2019, https://www.linkedin.com/pulse/women-being-liked-work-double-edged-sword-caroline-fairchild/

managers of our companies and our organizations at seeing that the men are reaching for opportunities more than women?[221]

Women in leadership need to actively sit at the table and be on the lookout for moments like these. Seek to notice when women are diminishing their accomplishments or reaching for further opportunities in leadership as it may not be as obvious in women when compared to their male counterparts.

Make your partner a real partner

Sandberg continues with her second point about making your partner at home an equal and practical partnership. She believes that there has been less progress in the stereotypes that perpetuate work at home compared to in the workplace. This has been proven by research with women performing three times the amount of childcare at home when compared to men. [222] Further to that, a study from Ohio State University found that men engaged more in leisure activities and while doing so, women were doing the housework 35% of the time. Comparatively, when women were engaging in leisure activities, men only spent 19% of the time performing housework. [223] This

---

[221] Sandberg, "Why We Have Too Few Women Leaders."
[222] Sandberg, "Why We Have Too Few Women Leaders."

[223] Claire M. Kamp Dush, Jill E. Yavorsky and Sarah J. Schoppe-Sullivan, "What are Men Doing while Women Perform Extra Unpaid Labor? Leisure and Specialization at the Transitions to Parenthood," *Sex Roles 78*, (2018): 715-730, https://link.springer.com/article/10.1007/s11199-017-0841-0

clear disparity between child rearing and housework has led to constant challenges for women in leadership, and it continues to characterize women's careers, family work and leisure time. [224] Sandberg points out that the job of a parent is one of the hardest in the world, and it's very important for people of both genders to see it as an essential job for both men and women. In order to "even things out and let women stay in the workforce," the perception around these at home tasks needs to change and men and women need to start contributing to these responsibilities and their partnership equally. [225]

Don't Leave Before You're Truly Ready to Leave

There is somewhat of a dilemma as Sandberg notes that the objective for women staying in the workforce can actually lead to their eventual leave. Meaning that, when women get pregnant or even when they get engaged, they begin to lean away from their work responsibilities and take on less projects. Women may begin to wonder how they can possibly fit children into their daily schedule and tasks of a demanding job.

---

[224] Dush, Yavorsky and Schoppe-Sullivan, "What are Men Doing while Women Perform Extra Unpaid Labor? Leisure and Specialization at the Transitions to Parenthood."

[225] Dush, Yavorsky and Schoppe-Sullivan, "What are Men Doing while Women Perform Extra Unpaid Labor? Leisure and Specialization at the Transitions to Parenthood."

Sandberg details what may happen next, "she doesn't raise her hand anymore, she doesn't look for a promotion, she doesn't take on the new project, she doesn't say, "Me. I want to do that."" Therefore, slowly moving herself away from leadership positions and quietly dodging the potential for advancement and more responsibilities. This can occur perhaps sooner than women in leadership may think. Sandberg notes an incident where a woman approached her regarding this topic, and she didn't even yet have a boyfriend. If you are not being challenged or rewarded by your work after you have "leaned back," it can create a self-fulfilling prophecy. You may not be taking the steps to be proactive therefore leading to less challenges and responsibility and therefore coming around to feeling like a leave, perhaps a permanent one, is the best and only choice. Sandberg says,

> If two years ago you didn't take a promotion and some guy next to you did, if three years ago you stopped looking for new opportunities, you're going to be bored because you should have kept your foot on the gas pedal. Don't leave before you leave. Don't make decisions too far in advance, particularly ones you're not even conscious you're making.

She strongly advocates that keeping women in the workplace is one of the most important factors in increasing the number of women in c-suite level leadership. It is crucial to note that even though a woman's tendency to "leave before leaving" may affect the dichotomy between a woman and a man's careers, organizations must also be responsible for cultivating women leaders by minimizing discrimination.

Senior staff attorney of the ACLU's Women's Rights Project, Gillian Thomas, speaks candidly about employers' views on pregnant women and new mother's abilities. "There is... more insidious forms of discrimination, where upon learning that you're pregnant, your boss begins finding fault in your work, or scrutinizing you more closely in order to try to find mistakes," she says. "and sometimes even portraying [their views] as benevolent concern – with statements like, "I figured that with a new one on the way you wouldn't want to work overtime," or "you'll fall in love with that baby and never come back to work." So even if a woman has not leaned back from her duties despite being pregnant, an employer could be the initiator in perpetuating these stereotypes that ultimately lead to less women in upper level management.

Some employers may not be willing to make accommodations for pregnant women or new mothers. This inflexibility leaves many mothers with difficult choices to make. Thomas notes that "an alarming number of employers refuse to make even the most modest job modifications...This leaves the pregnant worker in the conundrum of ignoring her physical needs (and possibly her doctor's advice) and continuing to work at full capacity, or leave the workplace altogether and losing her paycheck just when she needs it most." [226]

A woman's decision to leave her workplace cannot always be attributed to her own actions, just as it cannot always be attributed to the employer. Both companies and women in leadership alike should take the steps to ensure that women are not experiencing discrimination and harmful assumptions based around their pregnancy or new motherhood. Instead, women should seek to advocate for themselves, their responsibilities at work, and for what is best for them, their families, and their careers.

Building a Network

One of the most important aspects of cultivating women leaders and achieving continuous support on the journey to upper-level management or leadership is the creation of a network. Networking can be an intimidating process. The Center for Creative Leadership advised that many women within their program shy away from networking and even actively resist it. [227] It has been found that up to 85% of positions are filled through networking instead of

[226] Liz Elting, "Why Pregnancy Discrimination Still Matters," Forbes (Forbes Magazine, October 30, 2018), https://www.forbes.com/sites/lizelting/2018/10/30/why-pregnancy-discrimination-still-matters/?sh=4f698cc863c1

[227] "Do You Struggle with Networking? 5 Networking Tips for Women: CCL," Center for Creative Leadership, accessed November 27, 2020, https://www.ccl.org/articles/leading-effectively-articles/women-is-your-network-working-for-you/

through traditional job boards. [228] It was also found by McKinsey that relational assets make up 50% of an organization's intellectual capital while 75% of individual capital is the organizations' relationships. [229]

There are a variety of challenges that women encounter when trying to build a network as discussed in earlier chapters. Whether it be the exclusionary nature of the "old boys club," a lack of female role models, reduced confidence, or diversity barriers, women face a harder time when looking to build their strategic and professional networks. [230]

Five Key Strategies to Build Strong Networks

The following are five actionable strategies that can be used by women in leadership to build and further

---

[228] Sandy Hutchinson, "Study Reveals 85% of Jobs Filled By Networking," LinkedIn, May 22, 2017, https://www.linkedin.com/pulse/study-reveals-85-jobs-filled-networking-sandy-hutchison/

[229] That State of Human Capital 2012: False Summit, (McKinsey & Company, New York, 2012), https://www.mckinsey.com/~/media/mckinsey/dotcom/client_service/organization/pdfs/state_of_human_capital_2012.ashx

[230] Herminia Ibarra, "Why Strategic Networking Is Harder for Women," World Economic Forum, April 7, 2016, https://www.weforum.org/agenda/2016/04/why-strategic-networking-is-harder-for-women/

strengthen their networks despite the challenges that may come with it.

1. **Map your network -** To truly know the possibilities of your network, you may want to write or map it out on a piece of paper. Alternatively, you could use software like Canva or Visio to map it out in a digital flow chart. Draw a circle in the middle and write your name within it, and then write down the names of colleagues and friends and family with whom you have a strong connection. For connections that are not as strong, write their names farther away from the main circle. Then you may want to consider who you would like in your network who you have extremely limited connections with so far. You can write their name either as far as possible from the circle or on a separate piece of paper entirely. From there, seek to understand the patterns between your connections. Below are some factors you may want to consider for every connection:

    - Location
    - Function/Role
    - Their network and connections
    - Type of relationship

    Operational Connections: Related to workplace tasks and getting them done efficiently. These connections may include colleagues in management that are able to support and/or impede your projects. These are generally narrower in focus, and these types of relationships usually apply to one assigned task. Anyone who is involved in that assigned task and is contributing to its success should be a part of that operational relationship.

Personal Connections: Related to exchanging referrals and information. These types of connections should help with developing professional skills and can serve as mentor or role model relationships. You can look to expand this personal network through the participation in clubs, groups, professional associations, or communities that you hold a personal interest in.

Strategic Connections: Related to prioritizing, larger challenges, and stakeholder support. Where an operational network is narrow and focused on one task, strategic relationships involve connections to colleagues and stakeholders inside and outside your firm. They are associated with the ability to communicate, support and provide resources from one sector of a network to another in order to achieve results. [231]

---

[231] Mason Carpenter, Talya Bauer and Berrin Erdogan, "Personal, Operational and Strategic Networks," in Management Principles, (n.p., 2012), https://2012books.lardbucket.org/books/management-principles-v1.0/s13-04-personal-operational-and-strat.html

- Trustworthy
- Mutual benefits
- Diversity
- Recent or old connections

Once you've identified the patterns between yourself and your connections, you can begin to think about the strengths and weaknesses of your network and which connections may need some extra work and time invested in them. You may also find insight on who to ask for strategic introductions to those that you'd like in your network but are still out of reach. Identifying the gaps within your network and investing the time in building operational, personal and strategic relationships is especially important for women in leadership. By embracing networks as a key part in the process that engages other employees and leaders it can lead to a boost in the collective capacity for leadership. It can also lead to others within your network taking charge and stepping up when decisions need to be made about the future of a project or the organization itself. Finally, it can also cause a transformation of leadership culture. With a greater awareness of your network and how you fit within your organization, you can shift the reliance on command-and-control hierarchies to an active interdependent network instead. [232]

2. **Examine your Resources** - After mapping out your network, you should consider what resources you currently have in order to do your job effectively and potentially advance your career. The network map will help you identify your champions, mentors and sponsors that may help to forge your path as a woman in leadership. You may want to start with identifying what you need most from your network right now and then thinking about what you will need in the future from them. Next, you should seek to understand what resources your network already has and how you can access them. For example, if your short-term goal is to increase productivity in your team, and another manager in your strategic network has implemented an online project management system that has recently increased their team's production goals. Use your network to get in contact with this other manager to gain access to that resource. This may involve speaking with a personal connection to make an introduction or using facets of your organizational relationships to establish contact and to pool resources.

[232] "Network Perspective and Leadership: Are You Connected?," Center for Creative Leadership, accessed November 27, 2020, https://www.ccl.org/articles/leading-effectively-articles/networks-and-leadership-are-you-connected/

3. **Make Authentic Connections** - Networking is not all about systematic flow charts and using people for their applications, it is about connecting with the right people so that you have a greater insight and say in your future career. This comes with willfully working on emotional intelligence and active listening so that the relationships in your network are honest and sincere. This also can inspire others to have confidence in you as a woman in leadership if they feel that your relationship is genuine.

   As previously discussed, emotional intelligence is viewed as one of the most effective skills for leaders to have. Being emotionally intelligent can lead to higher levels of social astuteness, the ability to read and anticipate social situations. This can greatly benefit you when you are preparing for situations in which you need to make effective, sincere connections with your colleagues and employees. One way to bolster your social astuteness is to look for nonverbal cues of the people around you. In your next meeting, consider looking around the table to try and get a sense of your colleagues' emotions and how they are feeling, not just what they are saying. You can use active listening skills to not just listen but to understand how a person is feeling and where they are coming from. The six key active listening skills as outlined by the Center for Creative Leadership are:

- Paying attention
- Withholding judgment
- Reflecting
- Clarifying
- Summarizing, and
- Sharing.[233]

Even through mastering emotional intelligence and active listening, you still may need advice yourself. Any and all relationships should involve learning from others and sincerely listening to their opinions and what they may have to offer. According to research by Deloitte, employees value the potential growth of their career and the culture almost twice as much as they value their benefits and compensation. Their research also states that employees look for organizational cultures that focus on an environment of listening. [234] Dan Bobinski, a leadership training expert, says, "Millions of dollars are lost every day in organizations

---

[233] "Use Active Listening Skills When Coaching Others," Center for Creative Leadership, accessed November 27, 2020, https://www.ccl.org/articles/leading-effectively-articles/coaching-others-use-active-listening-skills/

[234] Global Human Capital Trends 2016: The New Organization: Different by Design, (Deloitte University Press, Toronto, 2016), https://www2.deloitte.com/content/dam/Deloitte/global/Documents/HumanCapital/gx-dup-global-human-capital-trends-2016.pdf

simply because of poor listening." Asking and listening for feedback is a critical step when building a network. If your connections do not feel as if you care to hear what they think then they won't offer you support and input when you may need it.

However, be careful to avoid developing biases and favoritism towards those that are closer to you in your network. Seek honesty from all of your peers as according to research from the University of Texas, supervisors have a tendency to develop "selective hearing when it comes to feedback."[235] The study found that managers tend to listen to those they feel most personally comfortable with; however, it leads to less listened to employees having lower performance reviews and it can erode the balance within your team.

4. **If you don't know, ask** - If you are feeling a bit lost in the complex development of your network, ask directly for networking tips from your supervisor or colleagues. This will also hopefully lead to receiving honest feedback about your networking style and how you are perceived by others as a leader. It is incredibly valuable to know how your employees view you and if your efforts may be coming off as insincere. If you are in the process of developing

---

[235] Rea Regan, "Workplace Democracy: What Is It and How Can You Create It?," Connecteam, August 23, 2020, https://connecteam.com/workplace-democracy/

a network, ensure that you always follow through on your promises to those connections. A lack of integrity will affect and possibly weaken your relationships if your credibility is brought into question. It can also undermine your influence as a leader.

After asking for and receiving honest feedback, it may be time to reflect on your networking strategies. You may want to keep a "network notebook" in order to write down your observations of interactions and connections that are strengthening versus weakening. If you've observed that certain connections seem to be isolating or weakening dramatically, you may want to create a list of the networking strategies that you've tried so far to identify the possible source of disconnect.

Knowing your employees and colleagues and becoming a wealth of knowledge to others is not only a successful management strategy but it is also immensely helpful when building up your network. If you are limited on resources, you can become the resource yourself. By becoming a hub of information, you can become a sought-after connection in other people's networks.

5. **Build, Maintain and Leverage -** As you work to strengthen the connections between your network consider two things: first, it will take time and you may need to be patient. Second, the value of networking is symbiotic. Once you have established what kind of network you

need and its specific goals, you should consider providing others with value before you require resources from them.

This may be information or sharing resources that you have in order to build relationships that have long term value. It is often thought that growing your professional relationships and connections involves attending formal networking events and conferences; however, you may also want to consider how to integrate your network into your daily or weekly work. This could involve making a network scheduling that may include strategies such as volunteering for new projects, asking for introductions to other connections, scheduling one-on-one meetings, or acting as a mentor. [236] You may also seek to have lunch or socialize with connections that are outside your closest circle and act as a connector for other employees and colleagues within your network. In order to fortify a strong network, you may need to push yourself to get out of your comfort zone.

Women in leadership can consider volunteering for projects or assignments that they regularly would not consider in order to strengthen not only their network but their skills in

---

[236] "Do You Struggle with Networking? 5 Networking Tips for Women," Center for Creative Leadership, accessed November 27, 2020, https://www.ccl.org/articles/leading-effectively-articles/women-is-your-network-working-for-you/

networking. The Center for Creative Leadership provides the following advice, "Just as relationships can be learned, so can the skills needed to strengthen your network. All are developed based on the concept that executives at any level must change the way they lead others by growing their relationships." [237]

The Differences between Men and Women's Network
The Most Crucial Networking Step for Women

The advice above is specific for women and women in leadership. According to research by the Kellogg school of management, women who attempt to build their network like men may actually do worse in the long run. [238] When men network, they tend to make larger and broader connections and they look to form alliances with their colleagues. The president of Leanin.Org, Rachel Thomas says, "I think men are socialized from the get-go to understand that mixing

---

[237] Center for Creative Leadership, "Do You Struggle with Networking? 5 Networking Tips for Women."

[238] Yang Yang, Nitesh V. Chawla and Brian Uzzi, "A Network's Gender Composition and Communication Pattern Predict Women's Leadership Success," *Proceedings of the National Academy of Sciences 116*, no. 6 (2019): 2033-2038 https://doi.org/10.1073/pnas.1721438116

business and friendship is what you do to get ahead. We, as women, aren't as comfortable doing that."[239]

Therefore, men generally are more comfortable in asking for what they want in networking with a clear business-oriented goal in mind. Men's networks focus on short-term need while women focus on building long-term connections and possible friendships. Because of this, women often have smaller networks that are based on trust as they make connections through people they know and that they feel comfortable with. Women may also seek to network for both personal and professional needs and therefore, trust perhaps becomes one of the most important factors within a women leader's network. This could also be why it may be easier for women to offer up their resources to others before asking for something for themselves. Women seek to leverage their relationships when creating a network interaction so even though they are generally more hesitant than men to ask for what they want, it could be because they are building up the trust of their connection first.

There are also several other factors that prevent women from networking like men. There may be challenges in socializing after work because of work duties at home that women are still primarily responsible for. There also may be a concern in

[239] Caroline Castrillon, "Why Women Need To Network Differently Than Men To Get Ahead," Forbes (Forbes Magazine, March 10, 2019), https://www.forbes.com/sites/carolinecastrillon/2019/03/10/why-women-need-to-network-differently-than-men-to-get-ahead/?sh=11881bfb0a17

networking socially in a male-dominated industry as women may be worried that their behaviour could be misconstrued. [240] And this goes both ways. Since the #MeToo era, the number of male managers that are uncomfortable with socializing, mentoring and even working alone with women in the workplace has increased by almost 15% in a year. [241]

Women in leadership should consider the following as the most crucial step when building their network: a close inner-circle of other women. Research has found after analyzing the social-network and job placement of those graduating from an MBA program, that the most important factor for men was how many highly-connected people they had in their network and how centralized they were within their own networks. This alone was enough for men to land top jobs; however, for women this was not the case. The most prosperous women required a tight-knit circle of other successful women. [242]

[240] Castrillon, "Why Women Need to Network Differently Than Men To Get Ahead."

[241] "Not Harassing Women Is Not Enough.," Lean In, 2019, https://leanin.org/sexual-harassment-backlash-survey-results.

[242] Yang Yang, Nitesh V Chawla, and Brian Uzzi, "To Land Top Jobs, Women Need Different Types of Networks than Men," Kellogg Insight, March 1, 2019, https://insight.kellogg.northwestern.edu/article/successful-networking-men-women.

The study by the Kellogg School of Management revealed that this is likely because of the critical information distributed on job opportunities. This information that's received may be related to opportunities for advancement, possible biases or discrimination in a potential workplace, and/or preparation for interviews.

The professor and coauthor of the study, Brian Uzzi says, "When you talk to women about their job interviews and the things that concern them, it's about how the culture of the firm is oriented towards women. That type of information is most helpful if it comes from another woman." And the results found that more than three quarters of the women that were the most successful had strong ties to two or three other women in their innermost circle. The study also found that those with this formidable inner circle of other women are nearly three times more likely to get a better job than women who don't. [243] Founder of Plum Benefits, Shara Mendelson speaks to her experience connecting and networking with other women,

> "I wanted to be respected as a
> business owner and leader, not as a
> woman who owned a business. But, I
> now realize that there are differences
> in the experience that only women
> can relate to... So I am making a

---

[243] Yang, Chawla, and Uzzi, "To Land Top Jobs, Women Need Different Types of Networks than Men."

concerted effort to associate myself
with women's resources."

Why Mentorship Is So Crucial

Over three quarters of American workers believe that mentorship plays a critical role in the development of an individual's career. However, only just over half of workers in America say that they have a mentor themselves. [244] There is a major gender discrepancy when it comes to mentorship. Despite it being viewed as such an important part of professional development, only 69% of women have had other women as mentors comparatively to 82% of men with male mentors. [245]

Neelie Kroes, Special Envoy, Start Ups NL believes that role models are the key to changing perceptions. She says, "It's the reality that when people picture a successful entrepreneur that can build and scale a business, they picture a man. It's also the reality that women themselves often assume certain things are not achievable or possible. A British documentary maker

---

[244] "Study Explores Professional Mentor-Mentee Relationships in 2019," Olivet Nazarene University, 2019, https://online.olivet.edu/research-statistics-on-professional-mentors.

[245] Olivet Nazarene University, "Study Explores Professional Mentor-Mentee Relationships in 2019."

summarised this perfectly: "If she does not see it, she can't be it.""[246]

Therefore, she cites women in leadership mentors and role models as being the critical missing piece in affecting the overall global perception and also as a key to breaking through barriers in male-dominated industries. Though inspiring women in leadership like Marissa Mayer and Sheryl Sandberg have been able to provide mentorship to potentially hundreds and thousands of women striving for professional success, there is still a lack of women in high-level management. But when organizations begin to place more women at the top of their organizations, this can begin to change the norm of what emerging women see and what path they may choose for their future. [247] Therefore, mentoring helps women to envision and ideate about their possibilities for their careers.

Mentors can also assist women in leadership with self-advocacy and taking charge of their goals. The confidence gap still affects women on a daily basis in that success has been correlated just as closely with confidence as it is with competence. [248] Mentors can

---

[246] Neelie Kroes, "'If She Can See It, She Can Be It'. The Importance of Female Role Models in Tech," HuffPost UK (HuffPost UK, July 16, 2016), https://www.huffingtonpost.co.uk/neelie-kroes/importance-of-female-role-models-in-tech_b_7809124.html?guccounter=2.

[247] Kroes, "'If She Can See It, She Can Be It'. The Importance of Female Role Models in Tech."

[248] Katty Kay and Claire Shipman, "The Confidence Gap," The Atlantic (Atlantic Media Company, August 26, 2015),

take some of the pressure off of women in leadership feeling that they need to constantly advocate for themselves in order to advance their careers. Though women in leadership should consider working on narrowing the confidence gap by building up their belief in their skills and abilities, mentors can provide a safe space for mentees to express their goals and ambitions.

Leaders in your organization may be unaware of the ambitions that you have; therefore, first expressing them to your mentor may provide some additional confidence to in turn share your career goals with your manager or supervisor. Mentors may also be able to provide personal experience on how they've navigated through the confidence gap and the glass ceiling to provide women with the insight they may need to maneuver through the process successfully.

The unfortunate reality is that for women in leadership they may have minimal options for other women to act as their mentors. This could mean that women looking for mentorship or sponsorship may need to instead look to influential male leaders. Organizations that are working to ensure that they are making the most of their talent should prioritize the mentorship and sponsorship of women from a variety of leaders.

You may want to consider what you need for yourself at this point in your career: a mentor or a sponsor. Both

---

https://www.theatlantic.com/magazine/archive/2014/05/the-confidence-gap/359815/

can be critical in helping to expand your network and advance your career, but there are some distinct differences between them.

Mentors vs Sponsors

At this point in your career, you may have already had a handful of people within your network that have helped to guide you. These may have been mentors and/or sponsors and while both are important there are some differences that should be considered when expanding your network, building a new one, or looking to become one yourself.

Mentors

Mentors provide support to their mentees by listening to their experiences and providing constructive and honest feedback. Mentors may provide this feedback around a specific need or for general ongoing professional development. A mentor can be an experienced employee at any level or role; a mentor does not necessarily have to be within a management position. They should provide guidance when the mentee needs to make choices related to their career and advancement. The relationship between mentor and mentee should be symbiotic in that both individuals will drive the relationship; however, the mentor should also be responsible for responding to an individual's mentorship needs. The actions that a mentor may take may involve helping their mentee navigate the path towards their career goals. This is why it is advantageous to pick a mentor who has had similar career and life experiences in order to gain information from someone who has forged that path before.

The Center for Creative Leadership has found that people who have mentors are better prepared for advancement and are more likely to be successful when promotions are available. They also will stay with their organizations for a longer period of time if they have a mentor, and they will score higher when performance is measured. [249] They also found that they have a larger impact overall within their organizations and have higher rates of resilience when encountered with challenges and setbacks.

Sponsors

The roles of a mentor and a sponsor may overlap, and a mentor may also label themselves as a sponsor. However, sponsors are more specific about the actions they take with their sponsoree and they usually will go beyond giving advice and providing guidance.

Sponsors will usually be a person within upper management or a senior leader within the organization. Their ultimate goal is to use their influence to help their sponsoree obtain the projects that they want and that are highly visible and be a

---

[249] "Why Mentoring & Sponsoring Are Important, Particularly for Women," Center for Creative Leadership, accessed November 27, 2020, https://www.ccl.org/articles/leading-effectively-articles/why-women-need-a-network-of-champions/

champion for their potential. This will likely also involve actively advocating for their sponsoree when advancement opportunities come up. The sponsor is the person who drives the relationship and they should continue to advocate for their sponsoree behind closed doors such as within executive-level meetings. A sponsor may push their sponsoree to take on assignments that are challenging and that will actively lead to breakthroughs in their careers. Since there is still a lack of women in c-suite level leadership, the pool of sponsors available to you in your organization may be primarily male. Though you may look for a mentor who shares similar career and life goals to you, this may be less important for a sponsor who is actively advocating for your career alongside you. This is because sponsorship is less about advice and guidance and more about actionable strategies and gunning for opportunities. Sponsorship may be a critical step for women looking to expand their network and advance their careers. Mentoring at all stages is important but the actions that sponsors take can assist women, especially women of color, who already have to overcome a multitude of barriers to reach their career goals. The Center for Creative Leadership advises, "Men in leadership roles are ideally positioned to strengthen the leadership pipeline in their organizations by helping to retain and advance talented women." [250]

If you are considering becoming a mentor or a sponsorship yourself, research around the Leaders'

---

[250] Center for Creative Leadership, "Why Mentoring & Sponsoring Are Important, Particularly for Women."

Counsel found that leaders who have become advocates for their employees have discovered a stronger commitment to their employer. They were perceived as better leaders by their employees, and they also found an increase in overall well-being including increases in job and personal satisfaction. [251] It also can lead to opportunities to scrutinize your own experience as a leader and the career path that you have laid out for yourself. It may contribute to the enhancement of stronger connections within your own network and to becoming a more effective leader overall.

Four Tips on How to Build a Mentorship Culture in your Organization

It is clear that mentorship can be a very important aspect that affects a variety of employees in a multitude of roles. As a woman in leadership, you may want to consider setting up your own mentorship program to help build effective leadership skills across your organization and to create possible avenues for your employees to achieve their career goals. The following are some tips for creating a culture of mentorship in your organization:

1. **Make it Company-wide** - When you are looking to open up a mentoring program, it may be tempting to only make this available within your department to retain ownership of the

---

[251] Center for Creative Leadership, "Why Mentoring & Sponsoring Are Important, Particularly for Women."

initiative. However, making mentorship available company-wide could be the most effective in order to facilitate cross-departmental collaboration. You may need to pitch this idea to upper-level management or receive approval from your colleagues. Every level of management should be involved in the decision and also within the mentorship program itself if possible or else your employees may be less accepting of this culture shift. One of the world's largest manufacturers of construction equipment, Caterpillar, has become a leader in mentorship culture across all of their departments. The mentors at Caterpillar provide guidance on nearly all aspects of their practices including, but not limited to, career exploration, development of soft skills, corporate culture, and work-life balance. In addition, all new hires are matched with a mentor for their first three years of employment, providing opportunities to try out different departments and find the best career-fit for that employee. The Vice President of Caterpillar's Large Power Systems Division, Tana Utley says "simply engaging purposefully with others in the interest of continuous improvement can spark positive growth...both personal and professional." In 2019, Caterpillar was named as one of America's Best Employers for diversity by Forbes and an excellence award for talent development in the same year. [252]

---

[252] "Awards & Recognition," Caterpillar, accessed November 27, 2020,

2. **Match Mentorships based on Skills and Role** - When you are looking to partner up mentors with mentees, it is important to look for soft and hard skills that may complement each other. Though personality should be considered, it should not be the only consideration when matching up employees. You should consider what value these employees can provide to one another and how their skills can effectively transfer to other positions or departments. This may involve looking for mentors that are highly qualified in both hard and soft skills that are needed to help the mentee develop. However, it is imperative to choose mentors with good communication and interpersonal skills in order to provide a supportive experience for both parties. You may also want to consider matching the mentor and mentee within similar departments and positions. Matches with transferable skills will likely produce the best results but the mentee and the mentor should be able to understand each other's roles and jargon. You might avoid communication problems if you match mentees with mentors that have similar functions within the organization. For example, if your mentee is within the sales department, you may not want to match them with someone in human resources. Career development firm, Insala advises that "similar departments and roles

https://www.caterpillar.com/en/careers/why-caterpillar/diversity-inclusion/awards-and-recognition.html give the mentee a long-term relationship with a mentor they will likely continue working with."

3. **Keep Track & Implement Structure** - If you are creating a mentorship that is organization-wide, it should be implemented with a trackable structure. After matching your mentees and mentors, it may be tempting to leave them to their own devices to establish a relationship. While it is important that they have an opportunity to take charge of the development of their relationship, those in leadership should ensure there is a structure in place for accountability. An evaluative component will ensure that the effectiveness of the program is maintained overtime.

   This can also assist with getting buy-ins from employees who may be more resistant to mentorship programs. Showing hesitant employees that the mentorship program can be successful based on observable data and positive feedback may assist with employee advocacy and acceptance of this new culture. As a woman in leadership, you may need to reinforce the importance of these developing relationships on a routine basis. You may need to consider creating designated spaces and times throughout the days and weeks to solidify mentoring relationships as an essential part of your organization's day-to-day-business.

4. **Build Communication & Trust** - Implementing a mentorship culture should challenge your

leaders and employees to practice their communication skills and actively discuss their career goals. As a woman in management, you should seek to be transparent with your employees and other managers about the mentorship program in order to gain their trust and faith in mentorship culture. In order to build up these communication skills and confidence in the program, you may want to speak with your human resources team in regards to confidentiality policies related to the mentor-mentee relationships. Confidentiality rules should be clearly stated to all employees on either side of the partnership. You may need to keep records of communication between mentors and mentees and all parties should be aware of where these records are held and why they are being kept. If necessary, you can create a formal agreement for mentors and mentees to sign off on but the policy in some form should be posted where employees can access it easily. It is also important to set out general roles and responsibilities of the mentorship program. For instance, the mentor should fill the role of a knowledgeable and experienced guide to the mentee. However, a mentor is not a counselor or therapist or career counselor. Ultimately, each mentor/mentee relationship should be treated with care and mutual respect.

Though women in leadership may need to approach networking and mentorship differently than men, establishing a mentorship culture and expanding your professional network is an important step in any professional's career. And though establishing a mentorship culture may seem rigorous and formal, it should be noted that women also have the option to establish informal mentorship relationships that can also be exceptionally effective. Heather Graham, ex-interior designer and stockbroker and current Director of Global Accounts for Asia Pacific gives the following advice:

> Mentoring does not have to be a formal agreement. Personally, my more successful mentoring relationships have been very informal. The key was that each of my mentors simply had my best interests at heart. They invested in my success without thought for their own interests. And, when I outgrew the available advancement opportunities within an organization, many of them mentored me right out of the company and into more advanced roles elsewhere.

Graham advises that mentorship will lead to more diverse workplaces and to organizations with more women in power. And she believes this all begins with you. She says,

> If you are a woman in a leadership position, make yourself known. Spread the word to all your colleagues and within your teams that you are happy to spend time

mentoring any of the women who are
interested in having a sounding
board. Or, if you prefer a more formal
structure, work with your human
resources team to set up an in-house
mentoring program.

Information Exchange: Talking Amongst Women

In September of 2020, Mrs. Imelde Sabushimike, the Minister of National, Solidarity, Social Affairs, Human Rights and Gender launched the information network project involving 50 million African women in Burundi. The goal of the project is to create a strong network of information exchange between women entrepreneurs through digital platforms that are already in place leading to their economic empowerment. This project has led to women across Africa receiving crucial business information about products sold by other women, as well as cross border exchange rates and prices.

Studies have shown that there is a digital divide and gender disparity between men and women when it comes to the use of Information and Communications Technology (ICTs). Initiatives like the one started by Minister Sabushimike can help reduce this inequality by providing women with communication platforms to initiate information exchange between women entrepreneurs and women in leadership. Minister Sabushimike believes that the use of ICTs has been one of the major driving forces of development in Burundi and that women play a crucial role in this development.

Information exchange leads to a sharing and knowledge about resources that women can use to advance their careers, facilitate the education of their children and to participate in the development of her nation. [253]

Information exchange is a benefit and important part of building out a professional network. It is also a driving force in developing nations to empower future women leaders and women in entrepreneurship. Information exchange amongst women has even been credited with increasing the overall quality of life in nations like the Southeast Asian country, Lao. Simple questions amongst Laotian women that involved, for example, asking a neighbor a question related to their health contributed to the improvement of an individual's overall well-being. [254]

---

[253] Jean de Dieu, "Launch of the Information Exchange Network Project among 50 Million African Women," ABP, October 1, 2020, http://abpinfos.com/launch-of-the-information-exchange-network-project-among-50-million-african-women.

[254] Kazue Sone et al., "Relationship between Active Information Exchange and the Quality of Life (QOL) of Women Living in Lao People's Democratic Republic," The Southeast Asian Journal of Tropical Medicine and Public Health 45, no. 4 (2014): 956, https://www.researchgate.net/publication/266136283_Relationship_between_active_information_exchange_and_the_quality_of_life_QOL_of_women_living_in_Lao_People%27s_Democratic_Republic

Research has found the women entrepreneurs and the managerial approaches of women tend to be more democratic and interactive. Women have a greater tendency to work collaboratively by sharing their knowledge and exchanging information. [255] However, there are several challenges when it comes to information exchange between women especially for those in developing nations. There may be a lack of information available due to limited access to digital platforms or to a professional network of women. There is also a lack of research on these issues that affect entrepreneurial women in developing countries.

The research that is available points towards social capital being one of the most important factors in information exchange. Men, in general, have better access to social capital than women. [256] This is especially true in rural areas, low-income areas and developing nations.

Further to this, though social capital may be essential for networking and advancing your career, it has been linked to an increase in stress in some areas. A study

---

[255] Irene Kamberidou, "'Distinguished' Women Entrepreneurs in the Digital Economy and the Multitasking Whirlpool," Journal of Innovation and Entrepreneurship 9, no. 3 (2020) https://innovation-entrepreneurship.springeropen.com/articles/10.1186/s13731-020-0114-y

[256] Enid Katungi, Svetlana Edmeades and Melinda Smale, "Gender, Social Capital and Information Exchange in Rural Uganda," CAPRi Working Papers 59, (2006), https://ideas.repec.org/p/fpr/worpps/59.html

performed in low-income areas of the United States found that establishing relationships for social capital actually led to an increase in mental distress and that it may be a source of stress for those living in economically deprived areas.[257] Women who are first beginning their careers or who may be from lower income households often encounter more challenges when trying to establish their professional network and build up their social capital. There was also a potential association found between social capital and depression when it came to analyzing these differences between men and women. Social capital had a significantly stronger effect on women when it came to experiencing symptoms of depression compared to their male counterparts. Particularly, this research found that for women in Moscow, Russia, trying to garner social capital outside their own family led to an increase in mental distress while family relations decreased the risk. [258] Therefore, gaining social capital outside your family may be intimidating and stressful. Women should be cognizant of these possible effects, but more research is required on these differences particularly when it comes to the association between social capital and health. There may be more

---

[257] Sara Ferlander et al., "Social Capital A Mixed Blessing for Women? A Cross-sectional Study of Different Forms of Social Relations and Self-Rated Depression in Moscow," BMC Psychology 4, no. 37 (2016), https://bmcpsychology.biomedcentral.com/articles/10.1186/s4 0359-016-0144-1

[258] Ferlander et al., "Social Capital A Mixed Blessing for Women? A Cross-Sectional Study of Different Forms of Social Relations and Self-Rated Depression in Moscow."

subgroups that are particularly influenced by this lack of social capital and that can be transcended beyond simply men versus women.

Nevertheless, the concept of social capital is another representation of gendered power within women's careers and everyday lives. Women have been able to sustain themselves in the face of male exclusion by building their own networks whether these are formed through their own organizations, digital platforms or local communities. [259] Throughout countries in Africa, women's networks and social capital building have been shown to enable women to pool their resources and protect their savings. In Columbia, women have been able to find negotiated solutions that allowed them to hold out against sexual violence by calling upon social capital through external employment. This use of networking and social capital has been developed for specific contexts as a reaction to external threats or power. [260]The process of building up your network and social capital could be in response to personal external threats that affect your career such as the glass ceiling, "old-boys network" or the double-bind dilemma. As discussed, women face a variety of challenges on their rise to corporate leadership. Therefore, social capital, particularly between other women, may be a key factor that is missing in order to

---

[259] Jane Franklin et al., "Women and Social Capital," (London South Bank University, April 2005), http://lsbu.staging.squizedge.net/__data/assets/pdf_file/0007/9439/women-social-capital-families-research-working-paper.pdf

[260] Franklin et al., "Women and Social Capital,"

break through these perpetuating challenges that women encounter.

Though women tend to be more democratic in their interactions as a manager, men are more inclined to pool information and use it to their benefit. This was confirmed by the World Bank who found that men's social networks are more formal with a greater focus on their careers while women gain their social capital through their families and communities. [261] Women are generally more dependent, especially in rural and developing areas, on informal networks and in forming collaborative networks that are based on geographical distance. This may be due to the fact that women have a high opportunity cost of time and the amount of time spent on information exchange is less if the contact is geographically close. [262] However, it has been shown that networks that are geographically close are limited in their scope and ability to exchange information. Men are more likely to expand their social networks and participate in civic engagement therefore providing them with greater access to information and fostering

---

[261] Nora Dudwick et al., Analyzing Social Capital in Context: A Guide to Using qualitative Methods and Data, (World Bank Institute, Washington, 2006), http://documents1.worldbank.org/curated/en/601831468338476652/pdf/389170Analyzin11in1Context01PUBLIC1.pdf

[262] Katungi, Edmeades and Smale, "Gender, Social Capital and Information Exchange in Rural Uganda."

the exchange of this information amongst their network. [263]

For women in leadership, this problem affects them especially disproportionately if they are taking on a large amount of family duties. Eagly and Carli theorize that women do not have the same access to social capital due to the fact that they are less likely to participate in office social events because of the work that needs to be done in their homes, for example, child rearing or housework, is too time-consuming. [264]

Therefore, it is of the utmost importance that professional women, organizations, and researchers work together to better understand the use of social capital when climbing the corporate ladder and specifically how this affects women and other marginalized groups. In 2016, findings by Natasha Abajian at the British Psychological Society's Division of Occupational Psychology annual conference, advocated for this by releasing research which concluded that professional women should better understand how to build, maintain and use social capital in order to be successful in reaching upper-level management. [265] Abajian advocated for the fact that

---

[263] Katungi, Edmeades and Smale, "Gender, Social Capital and Information Exchange in Rural Uganda."

[264] Alice H. Eagly and Linda Carli, "Women and the Labyrinth of Leadership," Harvard Business Review 85, no. 9 (2007): 62-71, 10.1037/e664062007-001

[265] "Ambitious Women Must Use Their Social Capital to Reach Top Jobs," ScienceDaily (ScienceDaily, January 5, 2016),

networking and social capital is responsible for a large percentage of career progression and yet women continue to have less access to these elusive networks that lead to career advancement. The research analyzed the responses from 12 women in c-suite level management and how they viewed social capital as an instrumental tool in their careers. However, the findings also revealed that all of the participants agreed that women lack the ability, knowledge, and opportunity to use this social capital and networks in the context of senior-level promotion. [266] Though Abajian says that she found it interesting to work with women who had broken through the glass ceiling, she warns and advises the following:

> I believe this phrase [the glass ceiling], by depicting a single obstacle at a high level, fails to account for the subtle inequalities that arise throughout a career journey. The continual use of this metaphor may encourage women to behave in a stereotypical gendered way rather than challenging the status quo. The participants in this study acted in a non-stereotypical manner and they succeeded in being appointed MD/CEO. Women who want to progress to the highest levels

---

https://www.sciencedaily.com/releases/2016/01/1601052239 52.htm.

[266] Science Daily, "Ambitious Women Must Use Their Social Capital to Reach Top Jobs."

need to be aware of the value of
social capital and know how to use
this to their advantage.[267]

Therefore, when you are looking to expand your networks and increase the value of your social capital, take your time to consider the individuals that align with your personal and professional objectives. Ericka Spradley, a career coach and Chief PowHer Officer at Ellevate, recommends soliciting individuals based on three set criteria:

"members, mindset and mutually
beneficial outcomes."[268]

1. **Members:** When looking to build your network, look for individuals and mentors who can provide you with example behaviors that you can model and who can expose you to further advancement or career opportunities. Also, as noted above, look to build a close-knit circle of women mentors as this has proven to be most successful for women who are looking to network. It would also be beneficial to choose individuals who can challenge your views and provide you with alternate perspectives when it comes to issues and barriers that you will encounter throughout your career. Therefore, your

---

[267] Science Daily, "Ambitious Women Must Use Their Social Capital to Reach Top Jobs."

[268] Ericka Spradley, "Social Capital Is 'The New Black,'" Ellevate (Ellevate), accessed November 27, 2020, https://www.ellevatenetwork.com/articles/9891-social-capital-is-the-new-black

network should have a balance made up of mostly women mentors, women in leadership who have experienced similar challenges to you and male allies or other allies that may challenge your viewpoints. All of these types of members can help to leverage your voice in leadership and provide clarity to your career goals.

2. **Mindset:** Spradley says, "aligning your relationships with your career goals should be a deliberate practice…" Women in leadership should look to include individuals in their network that share similar career goals to you and view career growth and acceleration in a similar way that you do. For example, if your goal is to strike the ultimate balance between motherhood and entrepreneurialism, you will want to look to include members in your network that empower this goal by having either done this themselves or by viewing it as an impactful and accomplishable task. While it is important to not get stuck within an echo chamber of opinions that are similar to your own, it is equally as important to separate yourself from other professionals that do not share the same growth-mindset as you. You may still be transitioning into a growth mindset yourself and this may be an arduous process that involves patience and self-reflection. However, Dr. Louis Spear, who provides mentorship for medical students, speculates that,

Mindset is not something that is static and unchanging, good news for people who want to cultivate a more growth-oriented mindset overtime or continue to reinforce their mindset as they move through the ups and downs of life... The fastest way to transition into a growth mindset is to surround yourself with people who have developed a growth mindset, and will continue to encourage and support you as you grow. [269]

3. **Mutually beneficial outcomes:** The final factor to consider when choosing individuals for your network after all of the contemplations throughout this chapter is whether the outcomes of your relationship will be beneficial for *both* parties. When you first initiate your network, you may find that your mentors provide you with an abundance of guidance and feedback that set you on the path to meeting your career goals. However, it is essential that your relationships, overtime, develop into ones that are reciprocal. Glenn Llopis helps companies build high-performance leaders and he says, "leadership requires relationships that add mutual value. The moment a leader takes the relationship for granted – there is no relationship." Llopis advises to look out for the following 5 signs in order to prevent a one-sided relationship that is headed in a direction that won't be beneficial for anyone:

   1. **They feel threatened** - They always have an excuse for not reciprocating work or

---

[269] Louis Spear, "How Do We Achieve a Growth Mindset?," MedChatMonday, February 22, 2019, https://medchatmonday.com/growth-mindset-definition/

networking. Look for signs of distancing and of territorial aggression.

2. **They lack relevance in the marketplace -** When they are not able to keep up with the needs of the marketplace, they are not able to reciprocate therefore potentially leading to the end of the relationship.

3. **They lack subject-matter expertise -** When your capabilities have exceeded expectations and the initial demands of your relationship, you may want to consider who is providing the information and expertise on the subject-matter. If you are constantly the only person contributing with well-rounded knowledge of your industry, you may want to re-evaluate your relationship.

4. **They lack collaboration skills -** This is the key point - If your mentor or ally is constantly only pushing their own agenda and is not willing to provide you with information and resources that benefit you, the relationship is not reciprocal.

5. **They lack appreciation -** "When you or the other side of the relationship begins to lose appreciation for what the other is trying to accomplish for the betterment of a healthier whole – respect quickly begins to fade," Llopis says. "If you can't find respect in a business relationship, you will never create and sustain

momentum together." [270] Therefore, showing your appreciation in a tangible way to your networks may be an important step to ensure that those around you feel your relationship is mutually-beneficial and respectful. [271]

---

[270] Glenn Llopis, "Relationships Without Reciprocity Are No Relationships At All," Forbes (Forbes Magazine, February 29, 2016), https://www.forbes.com/sites/glennllopis/2016/02/29/relationships-without-reciprocity-is-no-relationship-at-all/?sh=6e6ffd6b745e.

[271] Llopis, "Relationships Without Reciprocity Are No Relationships at All."

Chapter 6: CULTIVATE: How To Create Powerful Partnerships

Overview

As women in leadership you may already have several people come to mind when you think about male allies in the workplace. They may be mentors, sponsors, or advocates for equality when it comes to advancement and career goals of women. Alternatively, if you have a difficult time thinking of male allies in your workplace, it may be high time to ask the men in your office to step forward. It is especially true that male allies hold a great importance in male-dominated industries when women hold fewer executive positions and power. Research has also shown that male allies can serve not only as mentors and role models to women but also to other men.

Male Allies and Mentoring

Rachel Thomas says, "not harassing women is not enough. Being part of the solution means mentoring, sponsoring, and working one-on-one with women." As you now know, employees with sponsorship and mentorship are more likely to advance their careers.

Catalyst[272] and the Harvard Business Review[273] have shown that sponsored women are more likely to break through to higher levels of management. It was also found that women with sponsors are paid 10% more when compared to women without sponsors.[274] However, only 39% of women had held discussions with a mentor or sponsor in the last year when surveyed by the Working Mother Research Institute. Comparatively, over half of men had had conversations about their career goals with their mentor or sponsor. [275] It can be concluded that there still remains a disparity between women and men's access to sponsorship when looking to advance their careers. This could be due to a variety of challenges such as lack of women mentorship available, limited time to attend

---

[272] "Report: Sponsoring Women to Success," Catalyst, August 17, 2011, https://www.catalyst.org/research/sponsoring-women-to-success/.

[273] Sylvia Ann Hewlett et al., The Sponsor Effect: Breaking Through the Last Glass Ceiling, (Harvard Business Review, Brighton, 2010), https://30percentclub.org/wp-content/uploads/2014/08/The-Sponsor-Effect.pdf

[274] Teresa Perez, "Sponsors: Valuable Allies Not Everyone Has," PayScale, July 31, 2019, https://www.payscale.com/data/mentorship-sponsorship-benefits.

[275] The Gender Gap at the Top: What's Keeping Women from Leading Corporate America? (Working Mother Research Institute, New York, 2019), https://www.workingmother.com/sites/workingmother.com/files/attachments/2019/06/women_at_the_top_correct_size.pdf

social gatherings and minimal advocacy for her own career goals.

There are men who are willing to help narrow this gap. In 2019, a survey found that 87.5% of men wanted to help women to garner promotions and advance their careers; however, over half of the men were unsure how to help. Further to this, 49% of these men advised that they wanted their colleagues to give them advice on how to be a better ally to their female counterparts. [276]

Despite research finding that both men and women preferred to give and receive guidance in a one-on-one setting, few women are taking the steps to initiate a sponsorship or mentorship with a male superior. This especially occurs if it may subject them to after-hour meetings. There is a fear that women's motives will be misconstrued, and men share this same reluctance. Hewlett and the Harvard Business Review found that 50% of women looking to build their careers and 64% of senior-level men were hesitant to initiate any sort of one-on-one relationship with each other. [277]

---

[276] FairyGodBoss, "Engaging Male Allies." Powerpoint, July 2019, https://fairygodboss.com/presentation/male-allies-research

[277] Sylvia Ann Hewlett et al., The Sponsor Effect: Breaking Through the Last Glass Ceiling, (Harvard Business Review, Brighton, 2010), https://30percentclub.org/wp-content/uploads/2014/08/The-Sponsor-Effect.pdf

Brad Johnson and David Smith, authors of *'Athena Rising: How and Why Men Should Mentor Women'* advocate for a stronger relationship between men and women in the workplace in order to break through stereotypes and to see more women in executive level positions. Though they've received some pushback specifically from companies that feel they've already done enough when it comes to diversity and inclusion and encouraging male allies, Smith advises that organizations should consider the following questions:

> How do you know you've got this,
> that you're past this already? Have
> you asked the women that work in
> your organization? Have you done
> any sort of accountability measures
> and looked at numbers? I think that's
> the bigger broader question that lots
> of companies are looking at: How can
> I tell my people, the women who
> work for me in the organization that
> we're making good strides? [278]

As a woman in leadership, you should consider the above questions for your organization and your senior-level management. If you are having difficulties getting buy-in from your organization and from male mentors, it could be for a variety of reasons. Women cite some

---

[278] Meredith Hunt, "Male Mentorship Is Key Ingredient in Women's Success," Forté, September 9, 2019, http://business360.fortefoundation.org/male-mentorship-is-key-ingredient-in-womens-success/

major barriers when trying to establish male mentorship specifically when it comes to listening and gender stereotypes. Smith and Johnson interviewed many women with male mentors and the number one answer for improvement of their relationships was listening. They found that it was difficult for the mentors to actively listen in a quiet and empathetic way without looking immediately for a solution to the problem. The other main issue that women found with their male mentors was assumptions based on their gender. [279] It is clear that work needs to be done on both sides. Women should take the necessary steps to initiate a mentorship or sponsorship relationship if they feel it's beneficial for their career while men need to actively work on specific skills to provide more effective mentorship to women. Even if men do not want to take the actionable steps to become a mentor or if they are not in a position that allows them to do so, they can look to become an ally instead. Smith and John advise that being an ally to women is easy and simply involves being open to relationships, personal and professional. This could also mean that men may have to re-evaluate their views on gender bias and sexism which requires a certain level of self-awareness and openness to feedback. "The hard part is being willing to call out things in the workplace," Johnson says. "Especially on the part of other men. Men are more reluctant to advocate publicly for policies that are good for women, like pay differentials."

---

[279] Hunt, "Male Mentorship Is Key Ingredient in Women's Success."

213

77% of men believe that they are already doing all that they can to support equality between the genders. However, only 41% of women agree with this. [280]This could mean that men need to be more actively engaged in disrupting gender biases and sexism when these situations arise in their organizations. It was found by Catalyst that men will speak up, but it depends on two major overlapping factors: personal agency and organizational conditions. If the conditions of the organization include a climate of silencing, futility and combativeness then men are more likely to not speak up against sexism at work. However, men are more likely to speak up if they have a stronger personal agency that includes factors like their commitment to dismantling gender biases, their confidence, their awareness of the positive effects of speaking up, and their belief in their impact on the common good. [281]

Organizations may need to take some responsibility for their work climate when looking to increase male allyship and decrease possible incidences of sexism. Men should also look to educate themselves on the effects of sexism and harassment and build their

---

[280] *So, You Want to be a Male Ally for Gender Equality? (And You Should: Results from a National Survey and a Few Things You Should Know,* (Promundo-US, Washington, 2019), https://promundoglobal.org/wp-content/uploads/2019/03/Male-Allyship-Study-Web.pdf

[281] Negin Sattari, Emily Shaffer, Sarah DiMuccio, and Dnika J. Travis, *Interrupting Sexism at Work: What Drives Men to Respond Directly or Do Nothing?* (Catalyst, June 25, 2020), https://www.catalyst.org/reports/interrupting-sexism-workplace-men/

confidence in speaking up in volatile situations that affect women disproportionately.[282]

Johnson and Smith, however, believe that we will see an increase in male allyship by starting at home. Smith says, "We're not going to solve gender inequality without first being allies and equal partners at home, until men demand in the workplace the same opportunity for women that they have in their roles as partners, spouses, fathers, and parents."

Win with Male Allies in Male-Dominated Industries

No matter what strategies are used to increase male allyship in your organization, it should be considered that building these relationships and attitudes is especially important in male-dominated industries. With less women working in these industries, they face a multitude of challenges as discussed in Chapter 2. These are real, ubiquitous and pervasive problems that affect women in male-dominated industries and disproportionately affect women of color and people in minority groups. [283] In order to reduce these barriers

---

[282] Sattari, Emily Shaffer, Sarah DiMuccio, and Dnika J. Travis, *Interrupting Sexism at Work: What Drives Men to Respond Directly or Do Nothing?*

[283] Ethan Siegel, "6 Steps Everyone Can Take To Become An Ally In White, Male-Dominated Workplaces," Forbes (Forbes Magazine, October 25, 2019), https://www.forbes.com/sites/startswithabang/2019/10/25/6-steps-everyone-can-take-to-become-an-ally-in-white-male-dominated-workplaces/?sh=5cfa5a3249fd

and make these challenges more manageable, women need men to step up as allies and mentors that will take action. It has been shown that when women advocate for gender equality they are viewed unfavorably by their colleagues while it is the opposite for men. [284] Kim Stephens, co-founder of the Talent Strategy Institute, advises that "white males must be the target audience for change."[285] Stephens advocates that the majority will continue to silence the minority if leadership teams and organizations do not understand the benefits and corporate advances of diverse and inclusive teams. [286] Therefore, this becomes particularly important in male-dominated industries where the executive team is composed of mostly or entirely men. If a change in organizational culture and increase in male allyship begins with top-level management, buy-in is needed from male executives. There may need to be an entire organizational cultural shift in how roles are viewed and how mentorship and sponsorship is approached. Jonathon Rossiter, the Superintendent for Site Operations Centre at Oz Minerals speaks to working for equality in his organization as a male ally,

---

[284] Sarah Coury et al., "Women in the Workplace 2020," McKinsey & Company (McKinsey & Company, September 30, 2020), https://www.mckinsey.com/featured-insights/diversity-and-inclusion/women-in-the-workplace.

[285] Kim Stephens, "Male Allies Are Key to Diversity and Inclusion Challenges in HPC Industries," WHPC, August 5, 2019, https://womeninhpc.org/diversity-and-inclusion/male-allies-are-key-to-diversity-and-inclusion-challenges-in-hpc-industries.

[286] Stephens, "Male Allies Are Key to Diversity and Inclusion Challenges in HPC Industries."

I think it all starts with an acknowledgement that women are capable of doing any role that men can do, particularly in industries which have typically been male dominated in the past. We forget sometimes that just because a role has typically been carried out by a particular gender it doesn't rule out the other from succeeding in the same role - just simply remembering that everyone should be made to feel welcomed and have their voices heard.[287]

Male Allyship: Key Strategies & Examples

If you have taken the steps to form a partnership or mentorship with a male ally, you may want to consider some strategies for making this relationship as effective as possible. Much of this should fall on organizations themselves as the fostering of these relationships may include the implementation of policy change or new inclusive programs. For women in leadership, they should place responsibility on their male mentors to implement effective strategies for guidance; however, there are specific approaches that women may want to try in order to get the most out of these relationships.

---

[287] "Male Allies in the Workplace: Meet the Male Allies Working for an Equal Australia," *Work 180* (Blog), September 6, 2020, https://au.work180.co/blog/meet-the-male-allies-working-for-an-equal-australia

Strategies for an Effective Mentorship with a Male Ally

1. **Transparency** - When looking to schedule a meeting with your male mentor, do your best to ensure that these meetings are scheduled in public places and on your shared work calendar. It is best to avoid mentorship meetings in places like a bar or over dinner.

2. **Consistency** - Speak with other mentees that report to your male mentor. Ensure that you are receiving similar advice and offered help and that there is no discrepancy in the benefits that are shared between mentees. This really falls on the shoulders of the mentor themselves; however, you may want to set rules or guidelines in advance of your first meeting to ensure your goals are in line and that you will be receiving the same mentorship as others.

3. **Acknowledgment -** A successful relationship with your male mentor may involve acknowledging the difference between your experiences. Your male mentor may not be able to speak to your experiences as a woman in leadership in the workplace and your paths to advancement might be quite distinct. While it may initially be uncomfortable, it is important that you share your experiences with your male mentor. Jon Rambeau, Vice-President and General Manager at Lockheed Martin who was also named one of Aviation Week's 2012 Top 40 Professionals Under 40 in the global

aerospace industry says that he has learned a lot by inviting his women mentees to speak about their experiences in the workplace. Because of this, Rambeau has learned what women have had to compromise to fit in, and how much harder they've had to work to get to where they are.[288]

4. **Expansion** - Mentoring does not always have to be a long-term one-on-one relationship. There is still value in short mentoring sessions and surface-level conversations until deeper relationships can be established. In addition, if this is the first time you've had a male mentor, you may not yet feel entirely comfortable with one-on-one sessions. If this is the case, you may want to encourage your colleagues to form a mentoring circle instead. You can include both men and women under the guidance of a senior manager who can model the development of networking and relationship building skills. This is also an option for women mentoring other women. If you are a woman in leadership and just stepping into a mentorship role, you can try shorter sessions or group mentoring before establishing in-depth rapport with specific employees.

5. **Tangibility** - It is important to see how you and a male mentor could work together in a tangible way.

---

[288] Lisa Rabasca Roepe, "Why Male Leaders Should Mentor Women," SHRM (SHRM, November 26, 2019), https://www.shrm.org/hr-today/news/hr-magazine/winter2019/pages/why-male-leaders-should-mentor-women.aspx

You may want to come up with a project that you can work on together or ask your mentor to create one for the two of you. This could be especially advantageous at the beginning of a mentoring relationship in order to break down certain barriers and assumptions regarding how the two of you view and approach workplace projects individually. Relying on conversation alone may be a difficult start to a relationship between you and your mentor, specifically if the two of you have little in common outside of your workplace. The project could also be something volunteer based if you don't have any workplace projects that would work with your mentor.

6. **Accommodate** - As you build your relationship with your male mentor, you may consider some alternatives to traditional mentorship meetings. If you feel pressured or initially uncomfortable with meeting your male mentor in a one-on-one meeting or outside of work, you can ask your mentor to instead meet virtually such as through Zoom or Skype. You can put some responsibility on your mentor to come up with an alternative meeting place in which you will both feel comfortable and which will lead to a mutually beneficial relationship.

If you are a woman in leadership who is not looking for mentorship but is instead looking to implement mentorship into your own organization, you can consider some of the above points to help guide the implementation of male-female mentor and mentee relationships. However, in order to ensure equal support and guidance of men and women in your organization you may want to consider the following.

Firstly, the only way to ensure equal support is to track data and list employees who are being mentored and sponsored. Look to your senior managers and your colleagues for a catalog of their current mentees and sponsorees and compare the number of men, women and people of color. You may also ask your human resources department to develop a list of employees who are interested in becoming a mentee or a mentor. When cross-referencing these lists, scrutinize for any inequality between the sexes and marginalized employees. Alexis Krivkovich, a managing partner at McKinsey & Co says that organizations should look to shine a light on the possible inequities between their mentors and mentees.

Secondly, after identifying any gaps, recruit a group of women in leadership to help lead and establish goals for your mentorship program. If you are in a male-dominated industry, this is where you will need to seek out male allies or mentors to assist with championing. Set attainable targets for your program that are time-specific and measurable in order to determine the program's effectiveness over time. Your targets may include factors like an increased representation of women in management or the number of mentees that meet their advancement goals.

Perhaps, the best way to build a leadership and mentorship program for women in your organization is to look at an example of a successful program that was fully supported by an essential male ally: the CEO of American Express, Ken Chenault. The American Express: Women in Pipeline program began in 2008 with research on the company's diversity journey and the analysis of segments of their workforce to better understand how they could advance more women to executive-level management. At this time, American Express had many strong women leaders in mid-level management. Their research determined that capitalizing on these women in mid-level management could ultimately lead to them achieving their goal to have more women in senior roles. Therefore, the Global Diversity and Inclusion team introduced the Women in the Pipeline program. The program encouraged the development of sponsorship relationships between women and senior members as well as the creation of a women's network for sharing experiences and enabling ideas. [289] To create a more gender-intelligent organization, the program aimed to create more advancement opportunities for women by putting on their own conference, conducting focus groups, and individual interviews to identify possible barriers and opportunities affecting American Express employees. Their research into these barriers, published in the Harvard Business Review, included the following:

- Networking opportunities were more difficult to obtain for women
- Informal and direct feedback was harder to come by for women.
- Male behaviors dictated and characterized the organization's leadership culture

---

[289] Sylvia Ann Hewlett et al., *The Sponsor Effect: Breaking Through the Last Glass Ceiling.*

- As employees advanced, work-life balance became less available for both sexes
- Women lacked role models in senior positions, making it more difficult for them to envision their success
- As women advanced, they reported narrower requirements for senior positions that made them feel as if they had to fit a specific mold to succeed, and
- A lack of career mapping had left senior women confused about how to chart their potential advancements.[290]

Much of this would not be possible without the support of male allyship and specifically that of the CEO Ken Chenault. Male allies are especially important when they are the ones in senior positions that make the decisions regarding leadership programs like American Express'. Due to this program, its research and the combined efforts between male allies in senior leadership and dedicated women in mid-level management, more than 60% of American Express' employees are women. Further, more than 30% of the company's executives are women, twice that of the industry average. [291]

Kerri Peraino, American Express' Chief Diversity Officer says, "Because of the strength in our pipeline,

---

[290] Sylvia Ann Hewlett et al., *The Sponsor Effect: Breaking Through the Last Glass Ceiling.*
[291] Sylvia Ann Hewlett et al., *The Sponsor Effect: Breaking Through the Last Glass Ceiling.*

we're one of the companies best positioned to realize the benefits that gender balance can provide."

She advises that companies should work to create programs that intentionally create opportunities for women who don't have sponsorships and mentorships readily available. Not all sponsorships will turn into executive-level success, Peraino recognizes that "sponsorship has to be earned." However, this shouldn't stop women from taking the initial steps into a mentoring relationship as those first steps could be essential in determining your career goals and the overall culture dictated by your leadership teams. Peraino advises that it must start somewhere. She says, "we can do something to plant a seed, and that's what we're doing here." [292]

---

[292] Sylvia Ann Hewlett et al., *The Sponsor Effect: Breaking Through the Last Glass Ceiling.*

Chapter 7: WIN: How To Achieve Larger Gains with Negotiation

Overview

It is no secret that women in leadership experience a multitude of barriers in not only getting to their positions, but also in sustaining these positions as well. . When women are looking to advance or change organizations, they may need to negotiate certain aspects of their career such as pay, benefits and/or title. Sheryl Sandberg's advice is two words: "negotiate communally." However, there are several actionable strategies that women can try when negotiating that will hopefully prevent negative perception from the negotiators and lead to better results.

Why it's Harder for Women to Negotiate

Women tend to have more barriers and challenges than men throughout the negotiation process, no matter what type of negotiation is involved. Firstly, women are just less likely to ask for a raise. Linda Babcock, co-author of Women Don't Ask and economics professor, found that women requested raises about 30% less than men. Within a study of 78 students with their master's degree, Babcock found that only 12.5% of women negotiated their starting salary while 52% of their male counterparts did so. [293]

---

[293] Joanne Lipman, "Women Are Still Not Asking for Pay Rises. Here's Why," World Economic Forum, April 12, 2018,

In turn, this leads to an estimated $1.5 million loss of income throughout a woman's career. This loss and fear of negotiation that affects many women has been credited as being one of the driving factors behind the gender pay gap. In fact, although we are beginning to see the gap closing in certain industries due to the drive of younger women asking for raises, there are still disparate issues concerning negotiation between the sexes. For example, it was found in an Australian study that even when women were just as likely as men to ask for an increase in pay that they were still 25% less likely to receive it.[294] In this same study, they also found that younger women and men were "statistically indistinguishable," hence negotiating behavior may be changing for the better for future career women, with the younger generation stepping in and advocating for their salaries. [295]

Therefore, the reason why you may or may not be negotiating may depend on your age, it may also be based on your education. There was an especially steep gender pay gap revealed within positions that require the most education. Claudia Goldin, a Harvard labor economist, found that even when considering other

https://www.weforum.org/agenda/2018/04/women-are-still-not-asking-for-pay-rises-here-s-why/

[294] Lipman, "Women Are Still Not Asking for Pay Rises. Here's Why."

[295] Benjamin Artz, Amanda Goodall, and Andrew J. Oswald, "Research: Women Ask for Raises as Often as Men, but Are Less Likely to Get Them," Harvard Business Review, June 25, 2018, https://hbr.org/2018/06/research-women-ask-for-raises-as-often-as-men-but-are-less-likely-to-get-them.

factors such as hours, race and age, women doctors and surgeons earned 71% of what their male counterparts make. Women financial specialists are paid 66% less than male specialists. Women in Silicon Valley earn up to 73% less than men in the global center of high-technology. [296] This may be related to the large gap between men and women's negotiation skills when coming out of a master's program that Babcock discovered.

It's important to note that though there is a clear gap between men and women when it comes to negotiating pay or promotions, there are also barriers when it comes to smaller negotiations. Some smaller negotiations according to Harvard Business Review might include work resources such as gaining mentorship or sponsorship, restructuring teams, adjusting reporting lines or system upgrades. Professional development is another smaller negotiation that employees should consider when looking to re-evaluate their benefits and organization's culture. Finally, work-life balance, though viewed as a smaller negotiation, can still be quite impactful. In fact, this may be an essential conversation to have with your employer especially if you are a woman that is about to take a career break or go on maternity leave. These conversations can contribute to long-term career success and they may be an essential part of building your career as a woman in leadership. Negotiation works. According to Jobvite, 84% of those who are confident enough to take the steps to negotiate are

[296] Lipman, "Women Are Still Not Asking for Pay Rises. Here's Why."

successful. Further to this, about one-fifth of those negotiators saw their salaries raise up to 20%. [297]

So, if higher education is not the answer and negotiation has been proven to increase salary, why are women still not asking for more money?

Harvard Business Review interviewed 84 women about their negotiation experiences. These women mostly worked in metropolises and in large companies of over 500 employees. Negotiation was described by these participations as a "battlefield on which a lack of information or clarity on what you (or others) want is a disadvantage."[298] This is why it is essential to study up and develop negotiation strategies and competencies prior to entering these conversations. However, prior to developing these core competencies, it is also important to recognize the most common challenges cited by professional women. This will assist with the understanding of negotiations as a whole and challenges that you may encounter in these intimidating discussions.

---

[297] *2017 Job Seeker Nation Study: Finding the Fault Lines int eh American Workforce,* (Jobvite, Indiana, 2017), https://www.jobvite.com/wp-content/uploads/2017/05/2017_Job_Seeker_Nation_Survey.pdf

[298] Mara Olekalns, Ruchi Sinha, and Carol T Kulik, "3 Of the Most Common Challenges Women Face in Negotiations," Harvard Business Review, September 30, 2019, https://hbr.org/2019/09/3-of-the-most-common-challenges-women-face-in-negotiations.

Three Challenges Woman May Encounter when Negotiating

In this Harvard Business Review study, they identified the following three unique challenges that women may encounter during negotiations: "balancing self-advocacy and communality, managing difficult emotions," and, "overcoming interpersonal resistance."[299]

Challenge 1: Balancing Self-Advocacy and Communality

This first challenge is an example of the concept of the confidence gap which we explored in chapter 3, as outlined by Katty Kay and Claire Shipman in the Atlantic. Women are more reluctant to advocate for themselves in negotiation conversations. Many women in the HBR study pointed out that having the initial confidence to ask for what they wanted was challenging in itself. And if women do take the steps to ask, there is more fear surrounding possible backlash such as being seen as "unlikeable" or "pushy." In fact, women are twice as likely to be labelled as "pushy" than men.[300] Naturally, this is not the impression you want your supervisor and/or colleagues to have of you. Women looking for a raise or more benefits may be forced into this position where they have to choose

---

[299] Olekalns, Sinha, and Kulik, "3 Of the Most Common Challenges Women Face in Negotiations."

[300] Khazan, Olga. "'Pushy' Is Used to Describe Women Twice as Often as Men." The Atlantic. Atlantic Media Company, May 25, 2014. https://www.theatlantic.com/business/archive/2014/05/pushy-is-used-to-describe-women-twice-as-often-as-men/371291/.

between an increased salary or being liked. This lack of self-advocacy may also stem from a lack of mentorship or role-models within the organization. "As women, we don't have great role models when it comes to standing up for ourselves," a participant from the HBR study said. With this lack of mentorship, the fear of backlash and gap in confidence, women may have to be more aggressive to get the results that they want; therefore, choosing the backlash as the lesser of three evils. Another participant from the HBR said, "I had to basically point out that I manage people better than my male colleague...which goes against every part of what I would have liked to do." [301]

Challenge 2: Managing Difficult Emotions

The negotiation process is not an easy one and it can stir up feelings of reluctance and anxiety. This may be particularly true if it's your first negotiation where the results may be quite unclear and you may be afraid that it will end poorly. Despite women being, in general, more emotionally intelligent, they are also twice as likely to be affected by anxiety than men. It may also be even more difficult to maintain emotional composure when the negotiation itself brings up feelings of frustration and anger. When encountered with resistance, you may feel angry with the overall process and this can even lead to interpersonal conflict.

Another woman from the HBR study said, "when the negotiation didn't go well, I became angry. We got in a

---

[301] Olekalns, Sinha, and Kulik, "3 Of the Most Common Challenges Women Face in Negotiations."

big fight, if you want to call it that."[302] Situations like this will likely lead to damaged relationships, and it may prevent women from following up and asking for negotiations again in the future. Several women reported that a failed negotiation that led to negative emotions blocked them from making their asks again. [303] So, even if women are able to overcome their initial fear, they may be bombarded again with emotions that are more difficult to shut down. It may be important to try and detach yourself emotionally from your goals and desired outcomes when it comes to negotiation. In addition, emotions like anger and frustration are notoriously harder to hide. According to psychologist James Gross, response modulation is the last step in the process of generating emotions. However, response modulation is the step that allows people to change the intensity of their emotional reactions to increase or decrease its impact, for example hiding anger from your supervisor in a negotiation meeting. [304]

Challenge 3: Overcoming Interpersonal Resistance

The third challenge that women face in the negotiation process is the possibility of interpersonal resistance. There may be a concern that asking for a raise will

---

[302] Olekalns, Sinha, and Kulik, "3 Of the Most Common Challenges Women Face in Negotiations."
[303] Olekalns, Sinha, and Kulik, "3 Of the Most Common Challenges Women Face in Negotiations."

[304] Leanne Rowlands, "Emotions: How Humans Regulate Them and Why Some People Can't," The Conversation, October 19, 2018, https://theconversation.com/emotions-how-humans-regulate-them-and-why-some-people-cant-104713

affect your relationships with your supervisor and it is entirely possible that it will if it is not approached in a methodical and composed manner. Both men and women share this concern that asking for more money will negatively affect their relationships. 14% of women and 14% of men admit that this is a barrier to holding negotiation conversations. [305] Even if you are able to overcome this fear, you may get into your negotiation meeting and find that your fears were warranted. You may be met with different factions of resistance such as power plays, questioning of your competence and dismissal of your ideas. This will make it incredibly difficult to meet your goals for the session.

Within the Harvard Business Review study, many women provided examples for resistance during negotiation that included the following: "a manager missing a scheduled negotiation, showing horror and surprise at an ask, or being volatile and unpredictable in order to create uncertainty and pessimism."[306] All of these behaviors may be intended to discourage you from stating your needs and they may be effective in thwarting or stalling your negotiations all together. Resilience in the face of these obstacles is an essential skill. When you are met with aggressive interpersonal resistance, it may be tempting to step back. But many professional women who have participated in negotiations advise that these challenges should not be viewed as failures. Instead, they stress that

---

[305] Artz, Goodall, and Oswald, "Research: Women Ask for Raises as Often as Men, but Are Less Likely to Get Them."

[306] Olekalns, Sinha, and Kulik, "3 Of the Most Common Challenges Women Face in Negotiations."

"regrouping and trying again" is critical when met with resistance. [307]

If we can overcome these challenges, perhaps negotiation is the key to further narrowing the gender pay gap in the workplace. Carol Sankar, a leadership advisor and founder of the Confidence Factor for Women, says that "Women are not encouraged to perceive the value of developing an annual negotiation strategy without feeling penalized and judged. As a result, women will settle for lower compensation agreements and starting salaries." [308] It doesn't just fall on women to have these strategies in place but also on organizations and male allies to respond openly to negotiations from all employees. The solution is, theoretically, simple. If the cause for the pay gap is that women are not negotiating, then women must negotiate. Women must begin to ask for what they are worth and stop undervaluing themselves in the workplace.

Get Prepped: Game-Changing Negotiation Strategies

The following will discuss negotiation strategies for professional women. Perhaps the most detrimental mistake that women make prior to negotiating is a lack

---

[307] Olekalns, Sinha, and Kulik, "3 Of the Most Common Challenges Women Face in Negotiations."

[308] Carol Sankar, "Council Post: Why Don't More Women Negotiate?," Forbes (Forbes Magazine, July 13, 2017), https://www.forbes.com/sites/forbescoachescouncil/2017/07/13/why-dont-more-women-negotiate/?sh=4b08d43fe769

of preparation. In order to help you prepare for the conversation, consider these strategies:

Before the Conversation

1. **Join an Employee Resource Group (ERG)** - In order to prepare for your negotiation, you may want to speak with colleagues particularly women who have already experienced it. Therefore, you should consider joining an employee resource group to connect with other women who have had similar experiences. You may also find that ERGs will have expert speakers that provide valuable information about professional development, networking and negotiation. If your workplace does not currently have an ERG that suits this need, consider creating one within your organization by reaching out to your network or speaking with your supervisor. ERGs can be one of the first preparations in your step towards a higher salary or better benefits as they can provide constructive tailored information as well as potential mentorship opportunities.

2. **Consider Both Outcomes** - Prior to entering your negotiation you should consider that the first time you ask, your request may not be honored. Though it is clear that negotiation can be very effective with an 84% success rate, there is a possibility that you may encounter rejection. This is when your resilience and emotional intelligence will be tested; however, if you prepare for the possibility of a negative outcome you will be able to meet resistance in a more effective and composed

manner. Consider planning out a few words or phrases that you'd like to say if you are immediately shut down by your employer. Do your best to remain optimistic and resilient if you are rejected and begin working on improving your argument.

3. **What are you negotiating for?** - As discussed, there is more to negotiate than salary. Prior to entering any type of discussion, ensure that you have a good idea of what you are asking for. It could include work resources, professional development or more vacation days or better benefits. You may want to consider asking for more responsibilities that would better utilize your skills or you may want to ask for a sponsor to help advance your career. This could be the key to a large increase in pay in the long run as if you negotiate taking the lead within a department or on a project your argument will be more substantiated when you are looking for a promotion.

4. **Define your UVP** - Your Unique Value Proposition (UVP) is a statement that best describes your benefit as an employee, how you can solve your organizations or supervisors' problems, and what distinguishes you from your colleagues. Women notoriously underestimate their value. They apply for less promotions when they are more qualified than their male counterparts. [309] Women should

---

[309] Tara Sophia Mohr, "Why Women Don't Apply for Jobs Unless They're 100% Qualified," Harvard Business Review, August 25, 2014, https://hbr.org/2014/08/why-women-dont-apply-for-jobs-unless-theyre-100-qualified

work to determine their UVP prior to entering a negotiation. In order to do this, you must first think about how the person you are negotiating with perceives value. The better you understand what he or she views as valuable, the easier it will be to increase their perception of your value. In an ideal world, you should attach intrinsic value to your negotiation, meaning that you are offering your employer something that they want that won't cost you anything to give. Prior to negotiation, contemplate the following three things:

- **Your relevancy** - How can you solve key problems that your organization is currently experiencing? Consider listing relevant issues and your actionable strategies that will rectify these problems. Keep this list of issues minimal (2 or 3 major items) and your strategies straightforward to prevent your negotiator viewing your list as a reflection on their weaknesses.

- **Your quantified value** - What specific benefits and examples do you have that delivered quantifiable results? For example, if you led a project in the previous quarter that increased profits and/or productivity, obtain this data and prepare to share it in your negotiation.

- **Your unique value** - What qualities or results distinguish you from other employees in similar positions? This does not need to involve throwing other employees under the bus, but instead focusing on "I feel that-" statements that will clearly express what distinguishes you as a leading employee.

During the Conversation: Four Key Strategies for Any Negotiation

By the time you have actually entered the negotiation meeting, you should be prepared with the steps above to prevent a quick-turn around and rejection. There are a multitude of factors that may affect the way your negotiation meeting plays out but the following strategies can help prepare for the unexpected and keep your meeting on track.

1. **Start with Diagnostic Questions** - This is an important step that many negotiators miss. [310] However, perhaps the best way to present your benefits to your employer is to first find out exactly what they need and want from their employees and their organization. This can provide you with insight on which goals and aspects of your UVP that you should share in your meeting. You should already have an idea of what underlying issues are affecting your department but asking these questions may identify any that are viewed as particularly important in the eyes of your

---

[310] Victoria Pynchon, "Negotiation 101: Expert Advice for Getting What You Want," The Muse (The Muse), accessed November 10, 2020, https://www.themuse.com/advice/negotiation-101-expert-advice-for-getting-what-you-want

supervisor. These questions should always be open-ended, they will likely start with who, what where, when why and/or how. For example, "What do you think about the projected outcomes for this quarter?"

2. **Offer your UVP** - After you have established the needs of the organization and the individual that you're negotiating with, this is when you should offer your benefits and your unique value proposition. Do your best to express clearly and concisely the benefits that you have offered your company and your plan to improve these in the future. Remember to be specific about your organizational or department needs.

3. **Negotiate** - This is the part of the conversation where you may experience some resistance from your supervisor or interviewer and it is also where you may need to, once again, call upon your skills in resilience and emotional intelligence. If your supervisor has a different idea of your worth, counter their view with examples from your UVP, paying particular attention to the quantifiable results that you've already achieved. If your supervisor begins to get angry or unpredictable, consider the value of silence and of preparation. Resist the urge to interrupt with the facts that you've gathered and wait to express your points in an objective way. This will be a test of your emotional regulation. Anchor yourself by holding to the outcomes and goals that you came in the room with and keep your feet firmly on the ground. Victoria Pychon offered the following advice in the

Muse, "When you respond to insults with dignity, penalize your negotiation partner for his outburst with a proportional punishment, and quickly return to cooperation when he apologizes, you can turn your superior's harrumph into your triumph in short order." [311]

4. **Follow Up** - After you've come to an agreement that works for both parties, discuss the next steps. This may include factors such as discussing the agreement with human resources or another department. It should be clear who will be responsible for these discussions and when these steps will be taken. There is a possibility that your negotiation may be tabled for a different day if they want to consider a counter-offer or it may be interrupted, if this occurs set up an additional date and time to discuss your needs and consider sending an email with a reminder of this. If the negotiation was not in your favor, don't rush to set up another meeting. Re-evaluate the materials that you presented and consider if you require more quantifiable evidence to accomplish your goal. This may take some time to build up more evidence, but you can show your supervisor that you are still interested and firm about your negotiation if you take initiative on upcoming projects and work. If your negotiation was in an interview, you may need to wait for a counter-offer and this process will require patience. Do your best to stay in regular contact with the organization and keep the ball in

[311] Pynchon, "Negotiation 101: Expert Advice for Getting What You Want."

your court when it comes to communication by taking the initiative to follow up through email.

A powerful example of a successful negotiation for women in leadership is one involving an executive of a manufacturing firm by the name of Cheryl. This example is detailed in Deborah Kolb's book, Negotiating at Work.[312] Cheryl was near the top of her organization and she had spent 15 years distinguishing herself as a leader in international and financial management, mergers and acquisition strategy, valuation and structure. [313] When the position of chief financial officer in the company's supply division cropped up, Cheryl was the prime candidate for the job. Upon her acceptance of the offer, Cheryl packed up her family and moved to the headquarters in Texas. After two years in Texas, Cheryl's work-life balance was under threat as her family yearned to return to their home state. The manufacturing firm had little to no accommodations for flexible work in place at that point; therefore, Cheryl negotiated. She spoke with her supervisor and pitched him a formulated plan that included spending time at the organization's three different offices while still balancing her family life. This negotiation ended up being a win-win-win as it benefited the organization and her supervisor, her

---

[312] Deborah M. Kolb and Jessica L. Porter, *Negotiating at Work: Turn Small Wins into Big Gains* (San Francisco, CA: Jossey-Bass, A Wiley Brand, 2015).

[313] Nanette Fondas, "The Art of Negotiation for Women in the Workplace," Pacific Standard, May 5, 2015, https://psmag.com/economics/the-art-of-negotiation-for-women-in-the-workplace

family and herself. Cheryl did the work to express her unique value proposition and found a solution that provided advantages to all parties. And though this negotiation may seem small in relation to negotiations that lead to a raise or executive-level promotions, their value, however, cannot be disregarded. Cheryl's move into a flexible work arrangement allows the possibilities for her colleagues and employees to make the same negotiations for themselves. Nanette Fondas speaks to Kolb's book and Cheryl's situation in her article published in New America called, 'The Art of Negotiation." She says, "such small negotiations that occur daily in organizations can add up to a new negotiated order that makes room for more diversity in how people work."

Fondas and Kolb both advocate for negotiation culture in workplaces as they challenge the status quo and the barriers that are put up by traditional corporate work culture. Fondas says:

> So, if women and men decline to negotiate at work, they risk abandoning important opportunities to impact outmoded ways of working. They give up a chance to influence the negotiated order that defines their organization—an entity likely designed for a workforce that no longer resembles the people for whom it was originally a comfortable fit. The bottom line here is that to negotiate opens up the potential to achieve a small win for yourself that may engender a larger gain for others.[314]

---

[314] Nanette Fondas, "The Art of Negotiation," New America, April 23, 2015, https://www.newamerica.org/weekly/art-negotiation/

Conclusion

It is clear that women face a multitude of challenges throughout their careers so it's important to take advantage of opportunities to combat these persistent barriers rooted in bias and stereotypes when they present themselves. Whether it be due to gender alone or due to a combination of gender and other barriers marginalized groups face, women in leadership face great difficulties ahead as they try to forge a path for future generations. The goal of this book was to provide you as women in leadership with a guide to navigate these hurdles with actions you can take, strategies you can try, and networks you can form to become role models and trailblazers. Whatever your goal may be, whether it's to advance your career or to finally strike a work-life balance, working to develop yourself as a woman in leadership could lead to the betterment and amelioration for women in the workplace as a whole.

Bibliography

Adler, Lou. "New Survey Reveals 85% of All Jobs Are Filled Via Networking." LinkedIn, February 29, 2016. https://www.linkedin.com/pulse/new-survey-reveals-85-all-jobs-filled-via-networking-lou-adler/.

Adu, Aletha. "Piers and Susanna Row as He Calls Activist Greta Thunberg 'Unstable'." The Sun. The Sun, October 11, 2019. https://www.thesun.co.uk/news/10002266/greta-thunberg-piers-morgan-criticise-unstable-gmb/.

Ali, Carolyn. "Women in Business: Tackling Mental Health in the Workplace." Business in Vancouver, September 20, 2017. https://biv.com/article/2017/09/women-business-tackling-mental-health-workplace.

"Ambitious Women Must Use Their Social Capital to Reach Top Jobs." ScienceDaily. ScienceDaily, January 5, 2016. https://www.sciencedaily.com/releases/2016/01/160105223952.htm.

"The Art of Negotiation for Women in the Workplace." Pacific Standard, May 5, 2015. https://psmag.com/economics/the-art-of-negotiation-for-women-in-the-workplace.

Artz, Benjamin, Amanda Goodall, and Andrew J. Oswald. "Research: Women Ask for Raises as

Often as Men, but Are Less Likely to Get Them."
Harvard Business Review, June 25, 2018.
https://hbr.org/2018/06/research-women-
ask-for-raises-as-often-as-men-but-are-less-
likely-to-get-them.

Asplund, Jim, and Nikki Blacksmith. "The Secret of
Higher Performance." Gallup.com. Gallup, May
3, 2011.
https://news.gallup.com/businessjournal/147
383/secret-higher-performance.aspx.

"Awards & Recognition."
https://www.caterpillar.com/en/careers/why
-caterpillar/diversity-inclusion/awards-and-
recognition.html. Accessed November 27,
2020.
https://www.caterpillar.com/en/careers/why
-caterpillar/diversity-inclusion/awards-and-
recognition.html.

Babcock, Linda, Maria P Recalde, and Lise Vesterlund.
"Why Women Volunteer for Tasks That Don't
Lead to Promotions." Harvard Business
Review, November 22, 2019.
https://hbr.org/2018/07/why-women-
volunteer-for-tasks-that-dont-lead-to-
promotions.

Badgett, M.V. Lee, Holning Lau, Brad Sears, and
Deborah Ho. "Bias in the Workplace." Williams
Institute, June 2007.
https://williamsinstitute.law.ucla.edu/publicat
ions/bias-in-the-workplace/.

Baker, Joe. "How Good Leaders Manage Anxiety."
    TLNT, August 11, 2016.
    https://www.tlnt.com/how-good-leaders-
    manage-anxiety/.

Bhojwani, Sayu. "Why Women of Color Leaders Are So
    Tired." TwentyThirty, March 4, 2020.
    https://twentythirty.com/article/women-of-
    color-leaders-sayu-bhojwani/.

Bortz, Daniel. "Can Blind Hiring Improve Workplace
    Diversity?" SHRM. SHRM, March 20, 2018.
    https://www.shrm.org/hr-today/news/hr-
    magazine/0418/pages/can-blind-hiring-
    improve-workplace-diversity.aspx.

Boutelle, Clif. "What Is I-O?" SIOP News, March 12,
    2014.
    http://old.siop.org/article_view.aspx?article=1
    336.

Buchanan, Leigh. "All Leaders Have Anxiety. Here's
    How the Best Ones Deal With It." Inc.com. Inc.,
    May 8, 2018. https://www.inc.com/leigh-
    buchanan/anxiety-is-the-leaders-best-friend-
    and-worst-enemy.html.

Burkeman, Oliver. "According To 'Self Perception
    Theory,' Imitating Confident People Makes You
    More Confident." Business Insider. Business
    Insider, December 6, 2012.
    https://www.businessinsider.com/acting-
    confident-makes-you-more-conficent-2012-12.

Calhoun, Lisa. "30 Surprising Facts About Female
    Founders." Inc.com. Inc., July 6, 2015.
    https://www.inc.com/lisa-calhoun/30-
    surprising-facts-about-female-founders.html.

Castrillon, Caroline. "Why Women Need to Network
    Differently Than Men To Get Ahead." Forbes.
    Forbes Magazine, March 10, 2019.
    https://www.forbes.com/sites/carolinecastrill
    on/2019/03/10/why-women-need-to-
    network-differently-than-men-to-get-
    ahead/?sh=11881bfb0a17.

Chmura, Michael. "Venture Capital Funding Women
    Entrepreneurs Study." Babson College,
    September 30, 2014.
    https://www.babson.edu/about/news-
    events/babson-announcements/venture-
    capital-funding-women-entrepreneurs-study/.

Connley, Courtney. "Ambition Is Not the Problem:
    Women Want the Top Jobs-They Just Don't Get
    Them." CNBC. CNBC, March 5, 2020.
    https://www.cnbc.com/2020/03/05/why-
    women-are-locked-out-of-top-jobs-despite-
    having-high-ambition.html.

Cook, Vicki, and Amy Blacklock. "What Is The Best
    Advice For Returning To The Workforce?"
    Women who Money, October 19, 2020.
    https://womenwhomoney.com/best-advice-
    returning-work/.

Correll, Shelley J, and Caroline Simard. "Research:
    Vague Feedback Is Holding Women Back."

Harvard Business Review, April 29, 2016.
https://hbr.org/2016/04/research-vague-feedback-is-holding-women-back.

Coury, Sarah, Jess Huang, Ankur Kumar, Sara Prince, Alexis Krivkovich, and Lareina Yee. "Women in the Workplace 2020." McKinsey & Company. McKinsey & Company, September 30, 2020. https://www.mckinsey.com/featured-insights/diversity-and-inclusion/women-in-the-workplace.

Coyle, Daniel. *Culture Code: the Secrets of Highly Successful Groups*. New York, NY: Random House Business, 2019.

Dieu, Jean de. "Launch of the Information Exchange Network Project among 50 Million African Women." ABP, October 1, 2020. http://abpinfos.com/launch-of-the-information-exchange-network-project-among-50-million-african-women.

Dinc, Yilmaz. "How Far Have Immigrant Women Advanced in the Workplace?" Canadian HR Reporter. Canadian HR Reporter, March 8, 2019. https://www.hrreporter.com/opinion/hr-guest-blog/how-far-have-immigrant-women-advanced-in-the-workplace/298685.

"Diversity and Inclusion Initiative: A Step By Step Guide." TSNE MissionWorks, 2010. https://www.tsne.org/diversity-and-inclusion-initiative-step-step-guide.

"Do You Struggle with Networking? 5 Networking Tips for Women: CCL." Center for Creative Leadership. Accessed November 27, 2020. https://www.ccl.org/articles/leading-effectively-articles/women-is-your-network-working-for-you/.

"Do You Struggle with Networking? 5 Networking Tips for Women: CCL." Center for Creative Leadership. Accessed November 27, 2020. https://www.ccl.org/articles/leading-effectively-articles/women-is-your-network-working-for-you/.

Ellsworth, Diana, Ana Mendy, and Gavin Sullivan. "How the LGBTQ Community Fares in the Workplace." McKinsey & Company. McKinsey & Company, June 23, 2020. https://www.mckinsey.com/featured-insights/diversity-and-inclusion/how-the-lgbtq-plus-community-fares-in-the-workplace.

Elting, Liz. "Why Pregnancy Discrimination Still Matters." Forbes. Forbes Magazine, October 30, 2018. https://www.forbes.com/sites/lizelting/2018/10/30/why-pregnancy-discrimination-still-matters/?sh=4f698cc863c1.

"Establishing an Employee Resource Group." HRC. Accessed November 26, 2020. https://www.hrc.org/resources/establishing-an-employee-resource-group.

Fairchild, Caroline. "For Women, Being 'Liked' at Work Is a Double-Edged Sword." LinkedIn, July 31, 2019. https://www.linkedin.com/pulse/women-being-liked-work-double-edged-sword-caroline-fairchild/.

Fairchild, Caroline. "Nearly Half of Mothers Work, Take a Break, and Work Again. Why Is There Still Such a Stigma?" LinkedIn, March 4, 2020. https://www.linkedin.com/pulse/nearly-half-mothers-work-take-break-again-why-still-stigma-fairchild/.

Feldman, Chai R, and Victoria A Lipnic. "Select Task Force on the Study of Harassment in the Workplace." U.S. Equal Employment Opportunity Commission, June 2016. https://www.eeoc.gov/select-task-force-study-harassment-workplace.

Fondas, Nanette. "The Art of Negotiation." New America, April 23, 2015. https://www.newamerica.org/weekly/art-negotiation/.

Franks, Elizabeth. "Sexual Harassment in the Workplace." MEAA, January 29, 2018. https://www.meaa.org/news/sexual-harassment-in-the-workplace/.

Gabbatt, Adam. "Fox News Apologises to Greta Thunberg for Pundit's 'Disgraceful' Remark." The Guardian. Guardian News and Media, September 24, 2019.

https://www.theguardian.com/media/2019/s ep/24/fox-news-greta-thunberg-michael-knowles.

Gerhardt, Tilman, and Jens Riedel. "When Assessing Talent, the Essential Thing Is to Look at an Executive's Potential to Grow, Both Professionally and Personally." Potential: The Raw Material of the Future. Egon Zehnder, June 17, 2015. https://www.egonzehnder.com/what-we-do/executive-search/insights/potential-the-raw-material-of-the-future.

Gibson, Tim. "How Gay Women Are Treated in the Modern Workplace." myGwork. Accessed November 26, 2020. https://www.mygwork.com/en/my-g-news/how-gay-women-are-treated-in-the-modern-workplace.

Graf, Nikki, Richard Fry, and Cary Funk. "7 Facts about the STEM Workforce." Pew Research Center. Pew Research Center, January 9, 2018. https://www.pewresearch.org/fact-tank/2018/01/09/7-facts-about-the-stem-workforce/.

Graf, Nikki. "More Young Workers than Ever Are College Grads in U.S." Pew Research Center. Pew Research Center, July 27, 2020. https://www.pewresearch.org/fact-tank/2017/05/16/todays-young-workers-are-more-likely-than-ever-to-have-a-bachelors-degree/.

Graham, Ciera. "Barriers and Biases: 4 Challenges Faced by Millennial Women Leaders | Produced by Seattle Times Marketing." The Seattle Times. The Seattle Times Company, February 20, 2020. https://www.seattletimes.com/explore/careers/barriers-and-biases-4-challenges-faced-by-millennial-women-leaders/.

Grygier, Marek. "Struggling to Include More LGBT+ People? Remote Work Will Help!: Remote-How." Remote, June 2019. https://remote-how.com/blog/struggling-to-include-lgbt-remote-work-will-help.

Guttmann, Astrid. "U.S. Social Media Marketing Reach 2019." Statista, May 13, 2019. https://www.statista.com/statistics/203513/usage-trands-of-social-media-platforms-in-marketing/.

Harris, Stephanie. "Cultivating Women Leaders Creates a Better Workplace for Us All." Your Dream Blog, August 17, 2018. https://yourdream.liveyourdream.org/2018/08/cultivating-women-leaders-creates-a-better-workplace-for-us-all/.

Heathfield, Susan M. "How to Handle an Employee Sexual Harassment Complaint." The Balance Careers, July 13, 2020. https://www.thebalancecareers.com/how-to-address-an-employee-sexual-harassment-complaint-1916862.

Hewlett, Sylvia Ann. "Executive Women and the Myth of Having It All." Harvard Business Review, August 21, 2014. https://hbr.org/2002/04/executive-women-and-the-myth-of-having-it-all.

Hoffower, Hillary. "The US Birthrate Is the Lowest It's Been in 32 Years, and It's Partly Because Millennials Can't Afford Having Kids." Business Insider. Business Insider, May 24, 2019. https://www.businessinsider.com/us-birthrate-decline-millennials-delay-having-kids-2019-5.

Hudon, Tamara. "Immigrant Women." Government of Canada, Statistics Canada, March 3, 2016. https://www150.statcan.gc.ca/n1/pub/89-503-x/2015001/article/14217-eng.htm.

Hughes, Richard, Robert Ginnett, and Gordon Curphy. *Leadership: Enhancing the Lessons of Experience.* New York, New York: Mcgraw Hill Higher Education, 2014.

Hunt, Meredith. "Male Mentorship Is Key Ingredient in Women's Success." Forté, September 9, 2019. http://business360.fortefoundation.org/male-mentorship-is-key-ingredient-in-womens-success/.

Hutchinson, Sandy. "Study Reveals 85% of Jobs Filled By Networking." LinkedIn, May 22, 2017. https://www.linkedin.com/pulse/study-

reveals-85-jobs-filled-networking-sandy-
hutchison/.

Ibarra, Herminia. "Why Strategic Networking Is
Harder for Women." World Economic Forum,
April 7, 2016.
https://www.weforum.org/agenda/2016/04/
why-strategic-networking-is-harder-for-
women/.

Jagannathan, Meera. "How Do You Get Taken
Seriously at Work as a Young Woman?"
MarketWatch. MarketWatch, December 31,
2018.
https://www.marketwatch.com/story/how-
do-you-get-taken-seriously-at-work-as-a-
young-woman-2018-07-27-9884747.

Jay, Joelle K. "3 Ways for Women Leaders to Get Their
Work-Life Balance Back in Check." Inc.com.
Inc., October 25, 2016.
https://www.inc.com/joelle-k-jay/balance-
isnt-a-myth-3-ways-for-women-leaders-to-get-
their-work-life-balance-back.html.

Katen, Laura. "6 High-Powered Women Share Their
Secrets for Success." The Muse. The Muse, June
19, 2020.
https://www.themuse.com/advice/6-
highpowered-women-share-their-secrets-for-
success.

Kay, Katty, and Claire Shipman. "The Confidence Gap."
The Atlantic. Atlantic Media Company, August
26, 2015.

https://www.theatlantic.com/magazine/archive/2014/05/the-confidence-gap/359815/.

Kern, Merilee. "Expat Leadership: Lessons All Professionals Can Learn from Hugely Successful Immigrant Women." Thrive Global, July 10, 2019. https://thriveglobal.com/stories/expat-leadership-lessons-all-professionals-can-learn-from-hugely-successful-immigrant-women/.

Khazan, Olga. "'Pushy' Is Used to Describe Women Twice as Often as Men." The Atlantic. Atlantic Media Company, May 25, 2014. https://www.theatlantic.com/business/archive/2014/05/pushy-is-used-to-describe-women-twice-as-often-as-men/371291/.

Kolb, Deborah M., and Jessica L. Porter. *Negotiating at Work: Turn Small Wins into Big Gains*. San Francisco, CA: Jossey-Bass, A Wiley Brand, 2015.

Kroes, Neelie. "'If She Can See It, She Can Be It'. The Importance of Female Role Models in Tech." HuffPost UK. HuffPost UK, July 16, 2016. https://www.huffingtonpost.co.uk/neelie-kroes/importance-of-female-role-models-in-tech_b_7809124.html?guccounter=2.

Krogstad, Jens Manuel, and Jynnah Radford. "Education Levels of U.S. Immigrants Are on the Rise." Pew Research Center. Pew Research Center, September 14, 2018. https://www.pewresearch.org/fact-tank/2018/09/14/education-levels-of-u-s-immigrants-are-on-the-rise/.

"Leadership by Imitation." executiveexcellence.com, June 6, 2013. https://executiveexcellence.com/leadership-by-imitation/.

Lein, Simonetta. "10 Inspiring Women Entrepreneurs on Overcoming Self-Doubt and Launching Your Dream." Entrepreneur, July 13, 2020. https://www.entrepreneur.com/article/352948.

"Lesbian, Gay, Bisexual, and Transgender Workplace Issues: Quick Take." Catalyst, June 15, 2020. https://www.catalyst.org/research/lesbian-gay-bisexual-and-transgender-workplace-issues/.

Lipman, Joanne. "Women Are Still Not Asking for Pay Rises. Here's Why." World Economic Forum, April 12, 2018. https://www.weforum.org/agenda/2018/04/women-are-still-not-asking-for-pay-rises-here-s-why/.

Liptak, Adam. "Civil Rights Law Protects Gay and Transgender Workers, Supreme Court Rules." The New York Times. The New York Times, June 15, 2020. https://www.nytimes.com/2020/06/15/us/gay-transgender-workers-supreme-court.html.

Llopis, Glenn. "Relationships Without Reciprocity Are No Relationships At All." Forbes. Forbes Magazine, February 29, 2016. https://www.forbes.com/sites/glennllopis/2016/02/29/relationships-without-reciprocity-is-no-relationship-at-all/?sh=6e6ffd6b745e.

Luzio, Cate. "MeToo's Next Frontier: Addressing Backlash After Speaking Up." Forbes. Forbes Magazine, April 29, 2019. https://www.forbes.com/sites/cateluzio/2019/04/28/metoos-next-frontier-addressing-backlash-after-speaking-up/.

Mailk, Rasheed, Katie Hamm, Leila Schochet, Cristina Novoa, Simon Workman, and Steven Jessen-Howard. "America's Child Care Deserts in 2018." Center for American Progress, December 6, 2018. https://www.americanprogress.org/issues/early-childhood/reports/2018/12/06/461643/americas-child-care-deserts-2018/.

Martin, Erik J. "How to Handle a Sexual Harassment Complaint." https://www.uschamber.com/co, March 20, 2019. https://www.uschamber.com/co/run/human-resources/how-to-deal-with-sexual-harassment-complaint.

"Mental Health, Stigma and the Workplace." CAMH. Accessed November 26, 2020. https://www.camh.ca/en/camh-news-and-stories/mental-health-stigma-and-the-workplace.

Mohr, Tara Sophia. "Why Women Don't Apply for Jobs Unless They're 100% Qualified." Harvard Business Review, August 25, 2014. https://hbr.org/2014/08/why-women-dont-apply-for-jobs-unless-theyre-100-qualified.

Murrell, Audrey J., and Stacy Blake-Beard. *Mentoring Diverse Leaders: Creating Change for People, Processes, and Paradigms.* New York, NY: Routledge, 2017.

"Network Perspective and Leadership: Are You Connected?" Center for Creative Leadership. Accessed November 27, 2020. https://www.ccl.org/articles/leading-effectively-articles/networks-and-leadership-are-you-connected/.

"Not Harassing Women Is Not Enough." Lean In, 2019. https://leanin.org/sexual-harassment-backlash-survey-results.

O'Conor, Lottie. "Five Steps to Balancing Work and Family." The Guardian. Guardian News and Media, October 13, 2015. https://www.theguardian.com/women-in-leadership/2015/oct/13/five-steps-to-balancing-work-and-family.

Olekalns, Mara, Ruchi Sinha, and Carol T Kulik. "3 Of the Most Common Challenges Women Face in Negotiations." Harvard Business Review,

September 30, 2019.
https://hbr.org/2019/09/3-of-the-most-
common-challenges-women-face-in-
negotiations.

O'Neill, Brendan. "The Cult of Greta Thunberg." spiked
The cult of Greta Thunberg Comments. spiked,
May 6, 2019. https://www.spiked-
online.com/2019/04/22/the-cult-of-greta-
thunberg/.

Pace, Cindy. "How Women of Color Get to Senior
Management." Harvard Business Review,
August 31, 2018.
https://hbr.org/2018/08/how-women-of-
color-get-to-senior-management.

Parker, Kim. "Women More than Men Adjust Their
Careers for Family Life." Pew Research Center.
Pew Research Center, August 14, 2020.
https://www.pewresearch.org/fact-
tank/2015/10/01/women-more-than-men-
adjust-their-careers-for-family-life/.

Pereira, Shamanth. "A Simple Formula for Explaining
Your Career Gap in a Job Interview." Talented
Ladies Club, May 29, 2017.
https://www.talentedladiesclub.com/articles/
a-simple-formula-for-explaining-your-career-
gap-in-a-job-interview/.

Perez, Teresa. "Sponsors: Valuable Allies Not
Everyone Has." PayScale, July 31, 2019.
https://www.payscale.com/data/mentorship-
sponsorship-benefits.

Pynchon, Victoria. "Negotiation 101: Expert Advice for Getting What You Want." The Muse. The Muse. Accessed November 10, 2020. https://www.themuse.com/advice/negotiation-101-expert-advice-for-getting-what-you-want.

"Radical Candor - The Surprising Secret to Being a Good Boss." First Round Review. Accessed November 26, 2020. https://firstround.com/review/radical-candor-the-surprising-secret-to-being-a-good-boss/.

Regan, Rea. "Workplace Democracy: What Is It and How Can You Create It?" Connecteam, August 23, 2020. https://connecteam.com/workplace-democracy/.

Remes, Olivia. "Women Are Far More Anxious than Men – Here's the Science." The Conversation, June 10, 2016. https://theconversation.com/women-are-far-more-anxious-than-men-heres-the-science-60458.

"Report: Sponsoring Women to Success." Catalyst, August 17, 2011. https://www.catalyst.org/research/sponsoring-women-to-success/.

Ripton, Nancy. "Ten Simple and Effective Networking Strategies for Women." Diversity, October 10, 2019. https://diversity.rbc.com/ten-simple-

and-effective-networking-strategies-for-women/.

Roepe, Lisa Rabasca. "Why Male Leaders Should Mentor Women." SHRM. SHRM, November 26, 2019. https://www.shrm.org/hr-today/news/hr-magazine/winter2019/pages/why-male-leaders-should-mentor-women.aspx.

Rowlands, Leanne. "Emotions: How Humans Regulate Them and Why Some People Can't." The Conversation, October 19, 2018. https://theconversation.com/emotions-how-humans-regulate-them-and-why-some-people-cant-104713.

Royale, Africh. "Meet Chinwe Esimai: the Harvard-Trained Lawyer Passionate about Inspiring Generations of Immigrant Women Leaders ." Africhroyale, October 25, 2019. https://africhroyale.com/meet-chinwe-esimai-the-harvard-trained-lawyer-passionate-about-inspiring-generations-of-immigrant-women-leaders/.

Sandberg, Sheryl. "Why We Have Too Few Women Leaders." TED, December 2010. https://www.ted.com/talks/sheryl_sandberg_why_we_have_too_few_women_leaders.

Sankar, Carol. "Council Post: Why Don't More Women Negotiate?" Forbes. Forbes Magazine, July 13, 2017. https://www.forbes.com/sites/forbescoachesc

ouncil/2017/07/13/why-dont-more-women-negotiate/?sh=4b08d43fe769.

Sathiyanathan, Lakshine, and Lisa Xing. "An Accent Might Keep You from Getting Hired Even Though It's Not Supposed to, Advocate Says | CBC News." CBCnews. CBC/Radio Canada, January 23, 2018. https://www.cbc.ca/news/canada/toronto/the-accent-effect-toronto-3-1.4409181.

Saunders, Tracy. "The Return to Work Syndrome: The Unique Challenges Women Face Reentering the Workforce." TLNT, December 19, 2018. https://www.tlnt.com/the-return-to-work-syndrome-the-unique-challenges-women-face-reentering-the-workforce/.

Scott, Elizabeth. "How to Reduce Negative Self-Talk for a Better Life." Verywell Mind, February 25, 2020. https://www.verywellmind.com/negative-self-talk-and-how-it-affects-us-4161304.

Shellenbarger, Sue. "When Getting the Job Is the Easy Part." The Wall Street Journal. Dow Jones & Company, February 17, 2010. https://www.wsj.com/articles/SB10001424052748703798904575069590202587252.

Sheridan, Terry. "Millennials Now Make Up Largest Workforce Generation in US." AccountingWEB, November 17, 2017. https://www.accountingweb.com/practice/gr

owth/millennials-now-make-up-largest-
workforce-generation-in-us.

Siegel, Ethan. "6 Steps Everyone Can Take To Become
An Ally In White, Male-Dominated
Workplaces." Forbes. Forbes Magazine,
October 25, 2019.
https://www.forbes.com/sites/startswithaban
g/2019/10/25/6-steps-everyone-can-take-to-
become-an-ally-in-white-male-dominated-
workplaces/?sh=5cfa5a3249fd.

Singh, Sejal, and Laura E Dorso. "Widespread
Discrimination Continues to Shape LGBT
People's Lives in Both Subtle and Significant
Ways." Center for American Progress, May 2,
2017.
https://www.americanprogress.org/issues/lg
btq-
rights/news/2017/05/02/429529/widesprea
d-discrimination-continues-shape-lgbt-
peoples-lives-subtle-significant-ways/.

Skaggs, Chris. "Going Inbound for Talent Acquisition -
Glassdoor for Employers." US | Glassdoor for
Employers, July 18, 2020.
https://www.glassdoor.com/employers/blog/
going-inbound-talent-acquisition/.

Sneader, Kevin, and Lareina Yee. "One Is the Loneliest
Number." McKinsey & Company. McKinsey &
Company, January 29, 2019.
https://www.mckinsey.com/featured-
insights/gender-equality/one-is-the-loneliest-
number.

Spear, Louis. "How Do We Achieve a Growth Mindset?" MedChatMonday, February 22, 2019. https://medchatmonday.com/growth-mindset-definition/.

Spradley, Ericka. "Social Capital Is 'The New Black.'" Ellevate. Ellevate. Accessed November 27, 2020. https://www.ellevatenetwork.com/articles/9891-social-capital-is-the-new-black.

Stephens, Kim. "Male Allies Are Key to Diversity and Inclusion Challenges in HPC Industries." WHPC, August 5, 2019. https://womeninhpc.org/diversity-and-inclusion/male-allies-are-key-to-diversity-and-inclusion-challenges-in-hpc-industries.

Stephens, Pippa. "Women Bosses 'More Depressed' than Male Counterparts." BBC News. BBC, November 20, 2014. https://www.bbc.com/news/health-30127275.

Stop Street Harassment. "2018 Study on Sexual Harassment and Assault." Stop Street Harassment, February 21, 2018. http://www.stopstreetharassment.org/our-work/nationalstudy/2018-national-sexual-abuse-report/.

"Study Explores Professional Mentor-Mentee Relationships in 2019." Olivet Nazarene University, 2019.

https://online.olivet.edu/research-statistics-on-professional-mentors.

Sullivan, John. "Improve Retention Up to 50 Percent Because Post-Exit Interviews Get More Honest Answers." Dr John Sullivan, August 8, 2017. https://drjohnsullivan.com/articles/improve-retention-50-percent-post-exit-interviews-get-honest-answers/.

"Supportive Performance Management." Workplace Strategies for Mental Health - Supportive Performance Management. Accessed November 26, 2020. https://www.workplacestrategiesformentalhealth.com/managing-workplace-issues/supportive-performance-management.

Swiss, Deborah J., and Judith P. Walker. *Women and the Work/Family Dilemma: How Today's Professional Women Are Confronting the Maternal Wall*. New York: Wiley, 1994.

Tessier, Liane. "Why Women Don't Speak Out." Guts Magazine, April 29, 2015. http://gutsmagazine.ca/why-women-dont-speak-out/.

Tigar, Lindsay. "20 Inspiring Quotes and Mentorship Advice From Female Leaders." Real Simple, March 5, 2020. https://www.realsimple.com/work-life/life-strategies/job-career/women-mentorship-quotes?slide=662d05d3-1459-4a97-b6d8-2e34b1a917cf.

Tigar, Lindsay. "7 Female Leaders on How They Overcame Crippling Anxiety." Ladders. Ladders, March 3, 2020. https://www.theladders.com/career-advice/7-female-leaders-on-how-they-overcame-crippling-anxiety.

"Use Active Listening Skills When Coaching Others." Center for Creative Leadership. Accessed November 27, 2020. https://www.ccl.org/articles/leading-effectively-articles/coaching-others-use-active-listening-skills/.

Vozza, Stephanie. "The Discouraging Link Between Depression And Women In Power." Fast Company. Fast Company, January 15, 2015. https://www.fastcompany.com/3040484/the-discouraging-link-between-depression-and-women-in-power.

Walker, Aleia. "We Need to Talk About Being the 'Only One' in the Room." Skillcrush. Accessed November 2, 2020. https://skillcrush.com/blog/only-one-in-the-room/.

Washington, Zuhairah, and Laura Morgan Roberts. "Women of Color Get Less Support at Work. Here's How Managers Can Change That." Harvard Business Review, March 4, 2019. https://hbr.org/2019/03/women-of-color-get-less-support-at-work-heres-how-managers-can-change-that.

"The WANT Manifesto." WANT: Women Against Negative Talk, July 12, 2020. https://womenagainstnegativetalk.com/manifesto/.

Weisshaar, Katherine. "Stay-at-Home Moms Are Half as Likely to Get a Job Interview as Moms Who Got Laid Off." Harvard Business Review, February 22, 2018. https://hbr.org/2018/02/stay-at-home-moms-are-half-as-likely-to-get-a-job-interview-as-moms-who-got-laid-off.

Wellington, Sheila, Marcia Brumit Kropf, and Paulette R Gerkovich. "What's Holding Women Back?" Harvard Business Review, August 21, 2014. https://hbr.org/2003/06/whats-holding-women-back.

"What You Should Know: The EEOC and Protections for LGBT Workers." What You Should Know: The EEOC and Protections for LGBT Workers | U.S. Equal Employment Opportunity Commission. Accessed November 10, 2020. https://www.eeoc.gov/laws/guidance/what-you-should-know-eeoc-and-protections-lgbt-workers.

"Why Mentoring & Sponsoring Are Important, Particularly for Women: CCL." Center for Creative Leadership. Accessed November 12, 2020. https://www.ccl.org/articles/leading-effectively-articles/why-women-need-a-network-of-champions/.

"Women and Anxiety." Anxiety and Depression Association of America, ADAA. Accessed November 26, 2020. https://adaa.org/find-help-for/women/anxiety.

"Women Business Leaders: Global Statistics." Catalyst, August 11, 2020. https://www.catalyst.org/research/women-in-management/.

"Women Business Owner Statistics." NAWBO, 2019. https://www.nawbo.org/resources/women-business-owner-statistics.

Yang, Yang, Nitesh V Chawla, and Brian Uzzi. "To Land Top Jobs, Women Need Different Types of Networks than Men." Kellogg Insight, March 1, 2019. https://insight.kellogg.northwestern.edu/article/successful-networking-men-women.

Zalis, Shelley. "What You Need To Know About Taking A Career Break." Forbes. Forbes Magazine, January 30, 2018. https://www.forbes.com/sites/shelleyzalis/2018/01/30/the-truth-about-career-breaks/?sh=55eaf77e2a7d.

Zheng, Lily, and Alison Ash Fogarty. "Why You Still Have No (out) Trans People at Your Company." Quartz at Work. Quartz, June 18, 2018. https://qz.com/work/1308079/how-to-be-inclusive-of-trans-people-in-the-workplace/.